W9-DEZ-676

ASPERGER'S
AND
ADULTHOOD

QUICK START GUIDE

- Thinking about moving out on your own (if you haven't already) but not sure where to begin? See **chapter 1**.

- Finding a job can be challenging for anyone. **Chapter 2** offers advice for getting gainful employment.

- You're employed, but where will you live? Check out **chapter 3**.

- Dating is tough, even for neurotypicals, but it can be fun. Cruise through **chapter 4** for tips and tricks.

- You've got to have friends. **Chapter 5** talks about getting in on the social scene.

- We know you have questions and concerns. Flip to **chapter 6** for a collection of Q&As and scripts.

ASPERGER'S
AND
ADULTHOOD

A Guide to Working, Loving, and Living
with Asperger's Syndrome

BLYTHE GROSSBERG, PSY.D

Author of *Asperger's Rules*

ALTHEA
PRESS

CONTENTS

A NOTE FROM THE AUTHOR

As a learning specialist who has worked with dozens of talented children and teenagers with Asperger's, I'm excited about what the recognition and investigation of the autism spectrum will bring about in the next several years. I know firsthand the promise of children and young adults with Asperger's, and I'm convinced they will revolutionize the work world. In the next decade, about half a million Aspie adults will enter the workforce. That's a staggering number, but as awareness increases, and the Asperger's/high-functioning autism (HFA) diagnosis grows to include a broader spectrum, it makes sense. It's also worth noting that, in the decades since Asperger's became a recognized condition, countless people have been wading through adult life with Asperger's without a diagnosis. They, unfortunately, had to sort things out for themselves, and often struggled when it came to finding employment, love, and general stability in a world skewed heavily toward neurotypicals. Luckily, you don't have to. Within this book, I look at adulthood through the eyes of Asperger's syndrome and provide tips, tricks, and strategies to navigate some of life's challenges—from finding a place to live to pursuing and maintaining intimate relationships, and everything in between.

Even for neurotypicals, few things are more thrilling—or frightening—than getting out into the world. You've finished school or reached an age where you're itching for more independence. You can finally carve your own path, in whichever way you choose. For Aspies, though, this sometimes means leaving a well-established comfort zone. It also means (for better or worse) exchanging the security that comes from parents, teachers, or advisers—looking over your shoulder, telling you to go here, do this, or turn off the video games already—for a great deal more responsibility. It's a big challenge to find and keep a job, pay your bills on time, make decisions and advocate for yourself, and navigate through a world where everyone is not always able to understand your unique needs. But you're here with this book, informing yourself. And gathering information is a good first step to sound decision making.

In popular culture, there are false ideas about what people on the spectrum can and can't do. Add to those misconceptions the natural angst you have about the responsibilities you will face as an adult, and the future might not seem too bright. But the truth is, you can do pretty much anything you put your mind to, and the tools and strategies outlined throughout this book can help Aspies achieve what they are capable of. There is also a pervading myth that Aspies are somehow unfeeling, but nothing could be further from the truth. Aspies are sensitive people who just don't always play along with the world's often-arbitrary rules. As more and more Aspies enter the adult world, they will shatter these myths and make it clear to everyone around them that while Aspies may approach situations from different angles or express themselves in different ways, they possess deep emotions and enormous skills and talents.

Consider yourself a pioneer. You're a young adult in what is thankfully an era of increasing awareness. You've picked up this book, which is one of many tools and resources you will encounter along the way to help you maximize your success in the adult world. You have the brains, skills, and drive to make it happen. And the world around you is catching on!

BLYTHE GROSSBERG, PSY.D
BROOKLYN, NY

CHAPTER 1

What's Happening on the Spectrum?

While *Asperger's* is no longer the term used in the medical community (today, the condition is referred to as *high-functioning autism*, or HFA, or having an *autism spectrum disorder*, or ASD), there are many people who identify as having Asperger's—and who are rightly proud of it. Aspies, as people with Asperger's are sometimes informally known, are bright and have a lot of unique gifts to offer. By definition, Aspies possess above-average intelligence and generally have an area of great and compelling interest—whether it's words, math, music, sports, science, art, or animals, to name a few. However, people with ASDs often struggle with sensory issues, such as aversions to loud noises, bright lights, and unfamiliar textures. At times, they may be rigid and unwilling to change their schedule or outlook, and may struggle to understand social rules and interactions, particularly those of a spontaneous nature, leaving them feeling isolated, anxious, and often depressed. You may be familiar with a few of these and may possess your own particular issues.

Asperger's has only been diagnosed widely in the last decade or so, meaning that most people who are now diagnosed with ASDs are

In this book, I generally use the term Asperger's, or Aspies. While many people use this term to describe themselves, with pride, the medical community often uses the term autism spectrum disorder (ASD) or high-functioning autism (HFA). My usage of Asperger's throughout refers to and includes anyone on the autism spectrum.

young children, teenagers, or young adults. As this new generation grows up and matures, we have the opportunity to follow their path from an earlier age and learn even more about targeted strategies to help people with ASDs become successful in the workplace and navigate adult relationships—and capitalize on the important skills and gifts they already possess. This chapter presents you with some ideas about what you might face as you leave the nest, and some of the ways in which you can use your talents to kick-start a successful, full, and rewarding adult life.

Growing Up vs. Being a Grown-Up

When you were younger, Asperger's may have been a lot to contend with. You might've had to learn to use headphones during school concerts or take frequent water breaks when there was a lot of noise in the classroom. Your teachers probably ran the gamut—some you remember fondly, those who embraced your uniqueness, and maybe others deservedly faced the wrath of your Sharpie blackening out their teeth in the school yearbook. Your parents may also have done a lot for you, such as helping you speak with your teachers if you felt shy or buying or choosing your clothes for you.

By this point, though, you've probably found a routine and a way of life that works for you. You know what you like, and you are likely pretty masterful in the areas you're interested in—whether it's computers, music, art, writing fantasy novels, or anything else. You may have a good handle on the areas of life you enjoy, and you may have your life under control—because you're under your parents' roof. Fair enough. But what happens if you want to move out and find a job? What if you want to pursue a serious relationship? Maybe you have already moved out, so you're living on your own but feel obligated to get out more and socialize. In any case, adulthood presents its own set of challenges.

As we age, we find that we can no longer explain away behaviors that we could when we were younger. This is especially relevant for Aspies. For example, if you ate the same food every day in the high school cafeteria or loved speaking endlessly about video games, maybe your high school and even college friends accepted your behaviors. If you needed to take a certain train or bus to school, it was acceptable if you were late; even if your teachers and parents didn't love these behaviors, they accepted them and you got by. After all, childhood is a time to learn, and there was less on the line for you. You didn't have to show up at a job every day, and you very likely only had to tend to yourself and your own needs.

Yeah, things are different now. You might be realizing that you have to, or should, take on certain responsibilities that others used to shoulder. You might also need to consider how to change some old habits and even step out of your comfort zone to do so. If you are living on your own, you have to work to support yourself, so that's a must. And it includes getting to work on time, fulfilling your job responsibilities, and working with others, for starters.

If you're reading this on behalf of an Aspie friend or family member, kudos to you. Though the book is directed to the launching or newly launched Aspie adult, loved ones can gain a great deal from reading this guide. You'll come out with a better understanding of what Aspies go through to achieve full and rewarding adult lives, and better yet, you'll learn how you can play a key role in their successful launch!

SOCIAL SERVICES FOR ADULTS WITH ASPERGER'S

While many of the services provided for people on the autism spectrum are intended for children and their parents, there are also services available for adults with Asperger's. For example, in most states, there are non-profit organizations that provide training in adult skills and that offer support networks and social groups for adults with Asperger's. For more information, visit OASIS (Online Asperger's Syndrome Information and Support) @ MAAP at AspergerSyndrome.org.

In your younger years, maybe your parents introduced you to your teachers each year, and so all you had to do was nod and slip into your seat. If you forgot to hand in the work, maybe your parents contacted the teachers to explain your forgetfulness, and all you had to do was hand your teacher your paper without saying a word. But exit teacher, enter boss, and the game has changed. Don't worry, chapter 2 presents rules and tips for navigating key challenges in the workplace.

Then there are the things that aren't musts—like friends or romantic partners—but are pretty pivotal to a full and happy existence. Life is more interesting and we feel more connected if we have a social life. But yes, it's suddenly on you to make it happen. The way you lived when you were growing up might no longer work. Your parents perhaps played a role in arranging your social life. While you probably had friends and people liked you, perhaps your parents or siblings made connections for you. Your circle of friends might have been composed of people your family knew or others you had known for a long time—positioned right in your comfort zone. While it's important to keep up relationships with your old friends, it's rewarding to get to know new people who may share some of your current values, interests, and maybe even issues. Taking small steps to get accustomed to new settings in which you will have to get to know new people can bring a big payoff. Remember, the more you do something, the more easily it will come.

Flying the Coop

There are advantages and disadvantages to leaving home. Your parents may make meals for you, clean your room, and carry out the other chores, which allows you to spend your time at your leisure. And who can deny the financial benefits that come from living at home? But while this type of arrangement may seem desirable in many ways, is this truly allowing you to become the adult you want to be, and use the skills you've worked hard to develop? At some point, you probably learned how to do things such as clean your room, do laundry, make meals, and even make your own budget. But are you keeping these skills alive while living with your parents? Creating an agenda that builds on your responsibilities can help ease the transition to independence. With or without the input of parents or other trusted adults, develop a plan that includes tasks you will be responsible for—cooking meals several times a week, doing the laundry, or paying bills—and get comfortable with them before you move out.

Depending on your financial savvy, you may want to work independently or with your family to formulate a budget (see chapter 3 for a list of expenses to consider), open savings and checking accounts, learn how to reconcile your accounts, and learn more about adult financial responsibilities and resources.

While I frequently refer to "parents," make the term your own and apply it to whomever you feel is your primary caregiver. Perhaps it's a sibling, your grandparents, an aunt or an uncle, or a close friend.

What about dating or maintaining a vibrant social life? With a little effort, you are more likely to get out there and develop friendships and find a romantic partner if you are living on your own. Living with your parents might not allow for the freedom to come and go as you please, so you may not have the chance to develop those new relationships. Even if you have some privacy, the mere idea of others in the next room probably doesn't enhance the romantic experience for either partner. In addition, you may find that living at home reduces your motivation to work, especially if your parents are picking up the tab for the rent or mortgage and for food. To find—and stick with—a job, you might require the added motivation of having to pay your own way through life, or at least part of it, for starters. Ask yourself, is staying at your parents' house preventing you from reaching the accomplishments you know you are capable of?

No, leaving home isn't easy. It can be frustrating to find the right job and living space and to make enough money to support yourself. Most people in their 20s, including neurotypicals, find these goals difficult and sometimes even elusive despite their best efforts, and this launch to independence can be even harder for people with ASDs. While Aspies are very bright, they can often benefit from additional guidance and support to strategize things like how to get what they want, find a job, and build a social circle.

This book provides a road map for what you can expect when you leave home or graduate from college. It will point you toward the advantages and exciting points in the journey that you may not have considered, such as the freedom to come and go as you please, the chance to determine your own course, and the ability to spend your money as you'd like (after paying for expenses). More video games, anyone?

This book will also point out some potential obstacles and how to tackle them, such as understanding the rules of the workplace and the how-tos of making friends. Never mind for the moment if it sounds overwhelming. Does it intrigue you, even just a little? If so, start discovering step-by-step how you can use your unique gifts and talents to survive and thrive in this big wide world.

SOME COMMON CONCERNS OF THE ASPIE ADULT

Aspie adults generally have a strong sense of what they like and are comfortable with. It's good strategy to use this understanding of self to seek a career that capitalizes on what you like doing and are great at. But interpersonal relationships—how do you make and maintain them? Branching out from comforts like childhood friends to make new adult friends—especially those of the romantic variety—is key to a satisfying life. Success here depends on introspection and self-awareness, maybe working on reaction control or curbing the desire to talk about only certain subjects and focusing on give-and-take in the conversation as well as in the relationship. The workplace can be equally challenging, but its rules and expectations are sometimes more black and white. Adapting to change, being aware of responsibilities and deadlines, and learning social rules that can help you coexist, understand, and communicate effectively with a variety of colleagues—these can bring value to your work life. And it's important to learn how to advocate for yourself, avoid being manipulated or scammed, and keep in touch with your emotional well-being, seeking support when needed, no matter what your job is.

While this book provides some strategies to handle these common concerns of young adult Aspies, it's your life and you're in charge of it. As you read, think about what will work for you, and adapt the strategies to meet your needs.

CHAPTER 2

Off to Work, with Asperger's

According to the Centers for Disease Control, about 1 in 88 people are now diagnosed with ASDs. However, it's predicted that only 55 percent of people diagnosed with ASDs will have a job six years after graduating from high school. But the reality is, people with ASDs have a large number of talents waiting to be tapped. Consider this: Over the next decade, about half a million people with an ASD diagnosis will enter the workforce. These adult Aspies will bring tremendous skills and gifts to their jobs. In many ways, having Asperger's can be an advantage in the right workplace. Having Asperger's can even put you well ahead of the pack, as long as you find the right job and keep it. After all, you are likely detail oriented, interested in what you do, conscientious, and loyal. These are all qualities that employers value and that can help you shine in the right career.

Olivia's Story

Olivia is a talented twenty-something artist who was diagnosed with HFA when she was 11. Olivia has always loved painting, drawing, and design. She knows she is smart, but she struggled in her high school math classes because she simply couldn't remember the necessary formulas and calculations. Art has always been her refuge, particularly in middle and high school when other kids bullied her at worst or, on a good day, ignored her.

When she went to college, she chose to major in education because she thought it would provide a more stable living than a career in art. She wound up doing very well in an educational program. She wrote papers that were meticulously researched and finely worded and continued into graduate school. While working toward her master's, Olivia worked as a student teacher, giving one-on-one attention to struggling middle school students, and she even suspected that some of the students had Asperger's. Her heart went out to them, and she felt even further drawn to teaching, now inspired to help children who reminded her of her younger self.

Sounds like Olivia was on the road to career success, right? But reality proved different than the dream job she had imagined. When she started teaching a middle school class on her own, Olivia wasn't prepared for the difficulties of managing the emotions and actions of 25 kids. She found that the kids did not respect her because she couldn't control their behavior. Unable to focus on the needs and emotions of so many children, Olivia found herself shutting down, and when this happened, she'd make the kids work independently at their desks. They even began treating her like the bullies she recalled from her own middle school experience.

After only a year of teaching, Olivia realized that despite her empathy for some students, she made a poor classroom teacher. Fortunately, she found a position working in a small firm as a graphic designer, a job better suited to her skill set, interests, and working-environment needs. Today, her daily work involves coming up with creative solutions to design problems and working mostly alone at her computer. She occasionally must meet with her supervisor, but the supervisor handles most of the client meetings. On some days, she can work from home, which lessens the stress and sensory input that can overwhelm her.

Although it was a tough lesson, by learning more about herself, including her needs and the environments in which she operates more optimally, Olivia found a career that builds on her interests and allows her to work without being overwhelmed by sensory and emotional input. Olivia has learned it's acceptable, and smart, to allow coworkers or her supervisor to handle responsibilities that don't suit her, such as client meetings. In return, she takes on more project-based work as a graphic designer—work for which she is well suited and at which she excels.

///

Translate Your Talents

If you are choosing or reevaluating your career, perhaps you are taking inventory of what you do well—and what you want to avoid in a job. Have you ever developed an unrealistic sense of what something would be only to arrive and be caught off guard? Maybe you joined a club in high school, then showed up and discovered it wasn't at all what you thought it would be? It's easy enough to quit a club, but we all go into a job hoping for a rewarding and lasting experience. It's helpful to know up front what a job entails, including how much time will be spent dealing with others' emotions or handling conflicts. Even some positions that seem to be task oriented may involve a lot of interaction with coworkers or clients. If you've had to handle these types of demands before, you probably know whether you can deal with them or if you'd prefer a position that involves less interaction with others.

How can you turn your skills into a career in which you'll thrive? Begin by considering what you are good at. Think about your interests and skills, and how you can realistically translate these into a position that is achievable within the foreseeable future. If you enjoy drawing, can you work or train as a graphic designer, photographer, or web designer? If you love video games, you may dream of getting a position as a game designer, and you may be one of the lucky ones to get this type of sought-after position now or in the future. You can also consider ways to apply your love of technology, such as becoming a computer programmer or IT specialist, or finding work in the medical field as an X-ray technician.

The important thing is to be realistic about the immediate future—especially if you have already moved out of your parents' place or would like to move out and need to support yourself. Although you should never give up on your dreams or long-term goals, sometimes you have to find work that will support you in the short term. For example, if you want to be a sculptor, you may have to work as a web designer or a data-entry clerk while you pursue art in your free time. Keep in mind, it's not forever—think of it as a means to get where you want to be.

Finding the Right Fit

Finding a job involves multiple steps. Sadly, we're not usually able to just walk into the company we want to work for and get a job. But we also can't just sit around and wait for a job to drop in our laps. Here are some common-sense steps that can help in searching for a job:

1. Consider your interests, talents, and the positions that build on them. If you're stumped about how to find a job in your area of interest, reach out to a career counselor, either at your high school or college or at a nonprofit organization dedicated to helping adults with Asperger's (see the Resources section at the

end of this book for more information). These people are ready to help, and they usually have connections to employers and other vital resources.

2. If, after consulting with others, you're still not sure how to proceed, consider taking one of the most valid career tests backed by research: John Holland's Self-Directed Search, which you can take online at Self-Directed-Search.com. The test asks you some fairly easy-to-answer questions about your interests and skills, and then it generates a report with information about potential careers that might be right for you. The cost to take the test and receive the report is $9.95. Based on the potential job ideas recommended by the report, you can carry out further research, either independently or with a friend or career counselor, to see if any of these jobs would be a good fit for you. Then expand on the possibilities. For example, if the report says you would make a good sportscaster, brainstorm some related careers that might be more immediately accessible (e.g., scorekeeper, camera operator, clubhouse hand, pro-shop employee, concessions worker, caddy—whatever captures your interest and maps to your experience level).

3. Use personal connections. There's a saying, "It's not what you know, it's who you know." That is, in addition to applying online (online job sites can be very useful), ask your friends, parents, neighbors, and former teachers if they know about any open positions, especially in fields you are interested in. There is nothing wrong with asking people if they know of openings, or even if they can meet with you briefly to discuss what it's like to work in their field. Many businesspeople appreciate the chance to become a mentor and help a young person move forward in their career. If you are invited to an "informational interview," keep in mind that it may not result in a job. Instead, it's a way to find out more about a career field or position. And it has value. Every connection you make has the potential to link you to what you are looking for. But make them remember you. After

speaking with people, be sure to thank them for their time and consideration with a handwritten note or an e-mail. You may also want to set up a page on LinkedIn so you can showcase your skills, connect with friends and colleagues, and let people know you are looking for a job. Once you have a job, connect with your new colleagues through LinkedIn. Otherwise, you can lose track of people, and those connections are gone. In a short time, you will have a great network of connections. Also, LinkedIn is not an intrusive site that requires any real socialization—you can simply use it as an online resource to keep track of your contacts.

4. If you go on an interview, first research what people wear to the office. Many industries, such as the tech sector, are very informal, but other offices require employees to dress more professionally. Even if the office permits wearing jeans, you may want to dress more formally for your interview, as you'll convey to interviewers that you are serious about the position. A popular concept in business is, if you want to be taken seriously, dress the part. You will not offend anyone by being slightly overdressed. Also, being showered and groomed is critical, no matter where the interview. If you are concerned about your appearance, check with a trusted friend for assurance that you look acceptable before you head to the interview.

5. Practice some sample interview questions beforehand. "Can you tell me a bit about yourself?" and "Why do you think you are a good fit for this position?" are two standard questions you may get. Think about a one- or two-minute answer to these and other general questions. Many interviews start with small talk, casual conversation about a general topic such as the weather. This breaks the ice and gives the interviewer a chance to gather a first impression. Here's what the beginning of an interview could sound like between Luke, a 22-year-old college graduate who is interviewing for a position as a web designer, and the supervisor who is interviewing him:

Interviewer: *Hello, Luke, and welcome. Sure has been hot lately.*

Luke: *Yes, it has. I hope it cools down soon. I'm excited to be here, so thanks for taking the time to speak with me.*

Interviewer: *Sure. Let's start with your telling me a bit about why you are qualified for this position.*

Luke: *Absolutely. I worked with a company last summer that designed web pages for small businesses, including a local hair salon and a pet store. I started with the client's ideas and built a site that has resulted in increased sales for them. Actually, I have a reference from my supervisor for that position.*

Interviewer: *Great. Do you know about our company and what we do?*

Luke: *Yes, I have read your website and spoken to the human resources manager, but I'd like to hear a bit more.*

While each job interview differs, here's what Luke did right and how he responded to common concerns and interview questions that might come up in your interviews:

- He made a bit of small talk about the weather before his interview started. While this talk isn't strictly related to the interview and may seem unnecessary, speaking about an unrelated topic such as the weather helps convey to the interviewer that he is friendly and able to carry on a spontaneous random conversation.

- He was able to speak about his experience and relate it to how it prepared him for the position to which he is applying. He was able to tie his work experience to concrete gains he made for the company he worked for.

- He showed that he did his research about the current company (which is a great idea), but he was still interested in hearing the interviewer speak more about the company.

6. After an interview, ask your interviewer if you can follow up with him or her. For example, you can say something like, "Would it be all right if I called you next week to check in on the status of this job?" You don't want to overwhelm the interviewer or check in more than once or twice, but definitely be prepared for the hiring process to take longer than you might think it should, as very few people are hired right away. If you don't hear back, don't despair. The company could take longer to hire than you expect, and it doesn't mean you aren't getting the job. It's definitely a good idea to follow up with the interviewer by writing a polite e-mail or letter thanking that person for their time and expressing your continued interest in the job. Many interviewers look for this, and they remember who did and who didn't follow up to acknowledge their time. Some people believe that showering a person with text messages or e-mails shows interest, but it's not wise here. Repeatedly bothering the employer will make you less—rather than more—likely to be hired.

7. If you have applied or interviewed for several positions but have not been hired, check in with a trusted friend or career counselor to see if they have any suggestions. You can also check with local Asperger's support groups to see if they offer career counseling or job search help. Even though online job sites are an easy, nonconfrontational way to seek work, you may find that you are relying too much on them. Online sites can have a lower success rate for the job seeker because there is often so much competition. Instead, you may want to check in with friends, former teachers, former bosses, neighbors, and other people you know to see if they have any job leads. For example, your friend may work in a company that has an opening, and they can recommend you. But don't get yourself down over it; each interview is a chance to practice for the interview that lands you a position.

ASPIE STRENGTHS

There are many areas in which Aspies excel. In fact, having a diagnosis of Asperger's or an ASD can place you well ahead of the pack. Here are some of the strengths common to people with Asperger's. Do any of these traits have you nodding your head?

- **Detail oriented:** People with Asperger's often recognize patterns and are very good at pinpointing data that does not fit into a pattern. As a result, Aspies are very detail oriented—usually much more so than neurotypical people. Aspies perform well in areas in which attention to detail is critical, such as computer programming, engineering, and library science. The fields of engineering and technology are filled with people who have Asperger's. In fact, many high-tech and engineering corporations recruit and provide internships specifically for people with ASDs, recognizing that their strengths help their employers fill some very specialized and high-level needs.

- **Intense concentrators:** Aspies can concentrate intensely on areas that interest them, allowing them to master and develop technical expertise in that area (such as fixing cars, computers, or other devices).

- **Tech savvy:** Tech wizards such as Mark Zuckerberg, founder of Facebook, are rumored to have Asperger's, and experts believe that Silicon Valley is filled with high-functioning adults on the spectrum.

- **Wordsmiths:** Many people with Asperger's love words, and they also enjoy the study and science of words. They are very skilled at work that involves the love and knowledge of words, such as writing and editing. Several living authors are on the spectrum, such as Temple Grandin, John Elder Robison, and Pulitzer Prize–winning music critic Tim Page, and experts believe that literary lions such as Lewis Carroll and Emily Dickinson may have had Asperger's.

- **Loyal, honest, and punctual:** Aspies aren't generally known to lie. They also tend to be punctual and conscientious, and they prove very solid and loyal employees for these reasons.

- **In tune with kids and the elderly:** Some Aspie adults find that they get along better with people in other age groups, such as young children and older adults. They often find their calling in positions that involve working with these age groups, such as early elementary school teachers or professions dealing with the elderly. Many Aspies find that they do very well as music teachers—this is an area of interest for many adults with Asperger's—while others work one on one with children or the elderly in fields such as music therapy, art therapy, and social work.

Looking, Finding, and Sometimes Settling

While you're looking, be aware of which positions are right for you and which jump out at you, and consider some of the jobs that are often good matches for people with Asperger's (these jobs are just ideas and may not be the right fit—you know yourself best).

Try not to be totally literal about looking for a job. For example, if you like art, you don't need to be a career artist—you can always do art in your spare time. Art-related jobs and hobbies come in many forms, such as photography, jewelry making, graphic design, or web design. Think about ways you can apply what you like to do, and consider jobs that use your talents. Keep in mind that it can take several months to find the right job, so if you need money in the interim, consider working in a coffee shop, walking dogs, or something that will help you pay the bills until a more permanent position comes through. We all need to settle once in a while. Your big break will come; in the meantime, the more you network, the greater the likelihood you'll find that perfect job.

Money and Benefits and Keeping It Real

While money may seem like your first concern while looking for a job, remember two things: First, a high-paying job doesn't matter if you're doing something you hate. And second, you may need to take a position in the short term that allows you to get experience before you ask for more money. If you are interviewing for a position, do some research online (with reputable sources) or with people who currently hold that position, and find out the salary range for that position. Remember that people with less experience are paid less, even if they are well qualified for the position. While you're interviewing, have in mind a reasonable figure that most likely represents the lower to middle range of the salary for that position. If you are offered a job, you can negotiate salary, but it should be squarely in the range offered for that position in your area and for someone with

VOCATIONAL TRAINING

Several organizations offer job training that provides job search and on-the-job skills for people with Asperger's. One of these organizations is Lime, at **LimeConnect.com**. Lime is a nonprofit organization that is "rebranding disability through achievement." It helps connect university students and alumni to internships and careers with its high-profile and prestigious corporate partners, and the organization also offers webinars that help provide job training and job-search skills. There are also state vocational rehabilitation (VR) programs that help people with Asperger's who need assistance getting or keeping a job. These offices are run by the Rehabilitation Services Administration with both federal and state money. To qualify for help, adults must prove that they have a mental or physical impairment that interferes with their ability to get and keep a job, and there are other criteria that VR programs require before providing help. More information about Lime and VR programs can be found in the Resources section.

your level of experience. As part of your pay package, consider the benefits that come with your job. Does it include health and dental care or provide matching contributions for a retirement fund? A lower salary can be offset by a good benefits package and might be preferable to a similar higher-paying job with no benefits. Many Aspies need medications and services, such as therapy, to help them with depression, anxiety, and other issues that come up. If you need services like these, look into the types of benefits the health plan for the position covers.

Ask Questions, Answer Questions

Aspies tend to like specifics when searching for a job, to make sure that all the elements of the position are a good fit with their needs and concerns. It is good to know what you're getting into. For example, you may be applying for a job as a reporter, but are you aware that your job will also require meeting with interview subjects, attending press events, and going to staff editorial meetings each week? In other words, a great deal of the job will involve dealing with other people—not just writing. In addition, if you struggle with sensory overload, ask questions so you can get a good sense of what your workspace will be like. Will you have to interact with lots of coworkers and clients in a crowded, noisy, open common space, for example?

As you apply for a job, ask the employer detailed questions about what the job entails. Don't worry about being inquisitive, employers like it when you show interest and concern for a potential job by asking a lot of questions. Here are some common questions that can help provide you with insight:

- Can you tell me what an average day looks like at this job?

- What are all the tasks I will be responsible for?

- Are there client or other regular meetings involved in this position?

- Do you know where I will be working, and can somebody show me the workspace?

- What are some the qualities of a person you think will be effective in this position?

Again, don't worry about appearing too nosy. If you pose a lot of questions at a job interview, the interviewer will interpret this as sincere interest in understanding—and doing well at—the potential job. The key to success here: prepare ahead of time. If you anticipate some of the interview questions, you can develop answers in advance.

This will take some of the stress out of the interview process. Here are some questions that you might be asked, along with some ideas of how to answer:

Can you tell me why you'd be a good fit for this position?

Ideas for answers: Before your interview, review the responsibilities and tasks listed in the job posting, and think about how your skills match what the job is asking for. You can write these down so you'll have them fresh in your memory for the interview. For example, if the job requires you to create fliers, you can talk about how you created fliers for your last employer, a club event, or even for a personal purpose. These don't have to be work experiences— any experience is relevant. For example, you can say, "I created fliers for my lawn-mowing business and got three new clients."

Can you speak a bit about your skills?

Ideas for answers: Think about how to talk about your skills in a realistic way that showcases your talents without bragging. For example, it's preferable to say, "In my previous job, I met all my deadlines, even for a large last-minute project," (which you can talk about in detail) rather than "I'm the most responsible person you've ever met." Avoid exaggeration, and back up what you say with concrete examples.

Do you have any concerns or questions for me?

Ideas for answers: Don't hesitate to ask questions about the daily routines and general responsibilities involved in the job. And don't feel that you *have* to reveal that you have Asperger's or an ASD (see Disclosing Your Diagnosis on page 41). You can frame your questions in a positive rather than a negative light. If sensory overload is an issue, try saying something along the lines of "I am very responsible about deadlines, and during busy or high-pressure times, I find that I work best in my own office or at home. Would that ever be possible in this position?" This way of framing the question elicits the same information as the more negative "I get really overwhelmed if there is a lot of noise or a great number of people around, so I'll need to work at home." If something is going to be an issue that you need to discuss, talk it over beforehand and get feedback from a trusted friend or family member on whether they think your request is realistic. The important thing is to avoid knocking yourself out of contention by making demands at this stage of the job search and interview process.

Some Good Jobs for Aspies

Many believe that Aspies fall into subtypes, and each of these types contains its own skill set. While experts differ on what these subtypes are, some Aspies feel they know their own subtype. Some Aspies consider themselves artists or visual thinkers, some feel they are verbal or nonverbal, and some love patterns (and, as a result, gravitate toward areas such as math, engineering, and music). Different subtypes will obviously find different careers to their liking. While there are countless potentially good fits out there and you can do anything you set your mind to, many experts consider the following careers to be good matches for Aspies with a college education:

- **Computer programming:** This career allows you to focus on creating codes and programs, without a great deal of human interaction. It also builds on some typical Aspie strengths, including strong pattern recognition and being tech savvy. And the demand for these folks is growing.

- **Photography:** This career involves aesthetic mastery, attention to detail, and technical skills, three areas at which many Aspies excel. And depending on your social comfort zone, you can find work ranging from photographing lively weddings to capturing sunsets in the most desolate regions of the world.

- **Engineering:** Experts have found that Aspies are overrepresented in the field of engineering, which builds on traditional Aspie strengths such as pattern recognition, mathematical manipulation, attention to detail, and comfort with technology. No, this is not a bad thing—we need engineers, and it's a great-paying job!

- **Writing, editing, and copyediting:** Some Aspies love words and writing, and many enjoy the detail-oriented, solitary work of editing.

- **Web page design:** This ever-growing field utilizes traditional Asperger's strengths, including art and design, technology, and attention to detail. Web design is a fruitful combination of creativity and technical ability.

- **Library science:** This field allows Aspies to build on their interest in the written word and involves the care and cataloguing of books. Library science also involves helping others find information in online and print sources—areas in which many Aspies excel. It is generally a lower-stress career that involves predictable and contained interactions with other people and great attention to detail. And for Aspies who get overstimulated, there aren't many places quieter or calmer than a library.

- **Accounting:** This career allows Aspies to use their mathematical and detail-oriented skills and involves minimal contact with people. However, this job can get busy around the tax season if you are working with personal taxes.

- **Music:** Many Aspies love the technical skill, artistry, and pattern recognition involved in playing music, professionally or as an avocation (this career is also open to people without a college degree). Aspies might enjoy related careers, such as acoustical engineering: the study, design, and analysis of sound.

Some large companies are realizing that people with Asperger's can provide the skills they need. For example, Microsoft, Freddie Mac, and Walgreens are some high-profile companies that have recently started pilot programs to employ Aspies. These companies are not employing Aspies just out of generosity; instead, they believe people on the spectrum provide them with the critical skills employers need to succeed in a world that prizes innovation and creative solutions.

- **Mathematics:** There are careers that allow Aspies to enlist their love of and skill with math, including mathematician, statistician, and actuary. Many mathematicians work for the federal government in relatively stable jobs in areas such as defense and at places such as NASA. These careers often involve predictable routines and minimal client interaction.

- **Physics:** Many positions build on skills and interests in physics, including scientists and researchers. Some of these jobs are in the private sector, while others are with the government. These careers are also highly detail oriented and generally involve less social interaction.

- **Veterinary science (veterinarian, vet tech, or professor of animal science):** Famous autism activist and author Temple Grandin is an esteemed animal behaviorist whose deep understanding of animal behavior and fear has made her a revolutionary advocate for the humane treatment of animals. Related careers working with animals are attractive for Aspies who cherish, understand, and are often extremely gentle with animals.

- **Pharmacy:** Pharmacology is a well-paid profession that experts think will grow in coming years, as more and more Americans get older and rely on medications. Pharmacists dispense medication, keep track and notify patients of potential drug interactions, and keep detailed records. They must interact with customers, but usually in a straightforward way that involves answering technical and medical questions.

Here are other careers that can be a good fit for Aspies without a college education and for those who are relatively nonverbal:

- **Library assistant:** Many Aspies can find enjoyment shelving books, and some even memorize the numbering system and location of books, making them efficient and responsible on the job. And again, the library is a nice atmosphere in which to focus, especially for those who prefer the quiet.

- **Restocking associate:** Pick a store, any store; they all need restocking. Aspies have great memories and can easily remember where items go and restock them quickly.

- **Data-entry clerk:** Many Aspies have detail-oriented minds geared toward entering data quickly and accurately.

- **Lab technician:** Aspies have the accuracy and careful attitudes to be well suited to lab work.

- **Film editor, car mechanic, or computer repair person:** Aspies can often tackle any kind of job that requires technical expertise.

- **Craftsperson:** Many people on the autism spectrum enjoy, and are good at, jewelry design, sculpting, and related artistic fields.

Whether you are a college grad or not, there are countless jobs suited to Aspies (far more than those discussed here), and you may find a job inside or outside of these categories. Learn all you can by talking to people you know and reading up on the Internet. Ultimately, finding a job you love and can make a career out of is a really personal decision, and you should go with your strengths, your likes, and your gut. Many older Aspies have very strong opinions for and against particular careers. Some even complained that the "Aspie-friendly" field they entered turned out to be a poor fit for them. If you're considering a career direction, see if you can talk with or shadow somebody in that field to learn about the pros and cons before pursuing it any further.

Sticky Situations

Adults on the spectrum can sometimes run into trouble on the job because of their distinctive ways of acting and thinking—and sometimes it's because they have a hard time reading social cues and nonverbal forms of communication. Here are some common situations that can get you into trouble—and how to get out of them.

Choosing Battles Wisely

Colleagues inevitably have professional conflicts or disagreements, but if you know how to handle them, you've got one of the biggest work challenges under control. Aspies often have great independence of thought, like things done their way, and can be resistant to embracing an unfamiliar line of thinking. However, this type of rigidity can cause a situation in which you are seen as a troublemaker or a poor team player, and if you don't "drink the Kool-Aid," it can even result in dismissal from your position.

It is usually acceptable for you to gently state your honest opinion about a professional matter, but if you aren't in a position of power, you might have to let it go and accept that the boss may rule against you. Before you state your opinion, consider whether the matter is important or not—choose your battles. While we can often set up our home and personal life to our liking, many things in the workplace are definitely beyond our control, particularly for those just starting out. But with age, time, and seniority, you'll probably begin to find that your ideas become more respected, even sought after—a good reason to try to stick with a company—so you can build to that level.

Being Told What to Do: Ugh

"I love being told what to do," said nobody, ever. And because Aspies have great independence of thought and, often, a vision of what they want to do, it can be especially tough to follow directions, either because they know what the directions are and disagree with them—and thus disregard them—or because the directions are unstated or confusing. While you may have a keen sense of the ridiculousness of following the crowd, you will undoubtedly find yourself in situations that involve being forced to listen to and follow directions. Sometimes you need to follow these directions to keep your job. That's quite a consequence! If you continually find yourself having to follow directions that feel wrong or uncomfortable, it may be a sign that you are in the wrong position and that you may need to look for a new job. If you are at all confused about what to do, don't hesitate to ask for clarification from your supervisor.

Sensory Overload: Dealing and Discretion

You may find that you are feeling overwhelmed by noise, lights, crowds, or other sensory distractions at work. Though working at home is usually something that should be discussed in advance of accepting a position, it may be possible to ask your supervisor for the ability to work at home, at least some of the time, or to work in a quiet place. Try to avoid reacting to sensory overload by "stimming," or carrying out repetitive behaviors such as rocking, clapping, or tapping. If you need to stim, try to do it in a bathroom or another private place. If this is nonnegotiable, see if you can find a discreet stim method, such as rubbing your fingers together under the table or playing with a fidget toy, something that a lot of people play with at the office, like a stress ball.

Meetings: Staying Afloat in the Personality Pool

Meetings aren't just about the subject at hand. Meetings are interpersonal forums in which personalities come together, sometimes sparking innovation and creativity and other times generating heated discussions and discord. You may even witness a colleague's attempts to show superiority or put others down, speak over people, or force their viewpoint on the group.

Aspie or not, these meetings are stressful. If you find yourself feeling upset or defensive—or like your coworkers or clients aren't listening to you—you need a plan. The natural reaction might be to withdraw or become argumentative. But you can prepare for these situations. If you feel ready to lash out—or run out—perhaps you can put your head down and start taking notes. If nobody's paying attention, you can even discreetly write calming messages to yourself. Another option is to be armed with a few disagreement-diffusing one-liners like, "I understand your point," "I guess I have a different perspective," "I'll think about that," or "Maybe we can brainstorm some options."

If you choose to participate in a meeting by speaking up, a good rule of thumb is to limit your remarks to about one minute (unless you are making a presentation that is designed to go longer). If others become resistant to your ideas, it might be better to speak to them outside the context of the meeting. Often, people are less defensive when they are alone. Make your points—once—and resist arguing if others don't agree. That's a tough but important lesson for anyone in the workplace.

Then there are the socially unacceptable absolutes: making comments that are personal or harmful, or insulting or questioning a person's intelligence, ability, or appearance. These are always off limits. Without a doubt, nothing can be as maddening as spending eight hours in a room with an unpleasant person, but that's one of the challenges of workplaces around the world. The key is to find a way to work or disagree with a person, or walk away from an escalated situation without lashing out or insulting a person's character. Remarks like these are not only hurtful; others may interpret them as harassment, which can lead to dismissal even if you did not intend to harass the other person.

Another potential sticking point about meetings is that you may find it hard to keep up with the group and follow what's going on between the chatter, the inside jokes, and the distractions. If that's the case, ask a trusted coworker to fill you in after the meeting, or take notes so you can sort it all out after the meeting is over.

Finally, you may not see the point in making small talk—those seemingly meaningless conversations about the weather, sports, or what you did over the weekend—but others view it as a way to bond. Think of it this way: If you're in a workplace for eight hours, you potentially spend more time with your colleagues than you do with your family. So a sort of kinship forms, and people consider their workplace relationships a big part of their social life.

In order to participate in the small talk, it can help to learn a little bit about a local sports team or the upcoming weather. Make learning about subjects of small talk a study, as if you were studying history or computer code. Scan the news for the latest sports scores or for reviews of the latest movies, even if you don't really care. That way you'll know just enough to join the conversation. Keep your ears open for an appropriate time to add your thoughts. If you don't want to join in, you can still smile, nod, and let the neurotypicals do their thing without interrupting.

Bullying, Really?

Bullying at work is unfortunate and unacceptable, but it happens nonetheless. You may have been bullied when you were a kid. Well, adult bullies, like their younger counterparts, enjoy controlling others, but they may use different tactics. For example, they may threaten you with untrue statements, but more likely they will speak to you with a lack of respect or try to force you to do things that are really their job. The operative word here is *try*. The best way to defeat a bully is to forcefully tell them that you aren't going to listen to them. Firmly reply to their pushy ways with some of the following remarks:

- I need to ask you not to interrupt me when I am speaking with other people.

- How about you extend me the same courtesy you would like extended to you?

- If you need me to do something, I will have to clear that with my supervisor.

In addition, if you see a bully approaching your workspace, you can pretend to be quietly speaking on the phone. This tactic can work. The bully will get the hint and leave you alone. It may take several tries before the bully stops bothering you, so keep at it. If they try to interrupt you while you're on the phone, hold your hand up or mouth that you are speaking.

If your direct confrontation or avoidance measures don't work and the harassment continues, file a complaint with a supervisor or the human resources department. In the meantime, document these incidents, noting when the person has bullied you and what they said. This will be important evidence to share with a supervisor, and if a coworker witnesses this behavior, ask that person to back up what you say (and tell the supervisor there were witnesses).

The bottom line is, nobody can bully you if you don't allow it. Take away whatever power they think they have by simply standing up for yourself and refusing their demands. You are not in school anymore; you are all adults, and people are accountable for their actions. If somebody touches or even threatens you, that can be construed as assault.

Dealing with bullies can be challenging, as it requires advocating for yourself—a big step for less assertive people. But remember, bullies are cowards who seek an easy victim. And you're no victim.

Workplace To-Dos (and Not-to-Dos!)

There are some unwritten—and written—rules about workplace behaviors that you'll want to know. They will help you be successful. Here are some behaviors that *don't* fly in the workplace:

- **Making jokes or comments about people that attack or demean their intelligence, appearance, background, or group.** Coworkers will not only perceive these comments as insensitive, they also might interpreted them as harassment, which can lead to dismissal.

- **Referring to people's private lives or sexual identities.** Coworkers can interpret these remarks as harassment, too, and they could get you punished or fired.

- **Going into hysterics or having an emotional outburst.** This is not cool in the workplace. If you feel an outburst coming on, remove yourself and try to get to a private place or outside the office.

- **Exhibiting stimming behaviors.** Stimming will probably come across as strange or unprofessional to your colleagues. If you engage in these types of soothing behaviors, such as rocking, clapping, or tapping, use them in a private place, such as at home or in the bathroom, rather than in public.

These are some workplace behaviors you *do* want to adopt:

- **Return people's calls and e-mails on a regular basis.** Even if you don't think it's necessary to get back to someone, you should. One Aspie was fired from his job at a legal firm because while he was working to resolve an issue, he didn't respond to lawyers' questions about where he was in the process. He simply thought it wasn't necessary to respond until the problem was solved. However, neurotypicals usually expect you to get back to them, even if only to report that you are still working on something.

- **Think about the content before you send a note or e-mail or post something online.** You can't take these posts or e-mails back, and if they are rude or misinterpreted as rude, you can find yourself in hot water. If you need to say something difficult, say it in person so it does not create a permanent record. Of course, saying difficult things in person requires thinking before you speak. You might talk it over beforehand with a trusted friend or family member to get their insight.

- **Answer the phone and e-mails in a polite way.** To get an idea of what works, listen to the nicest person in your office. How does he or she speak to people on the phone?

- **If someone is speaking to you, avoid looking at your phone or computer.** Try to look them in the eye, at least occasionally.

- **Say good morning to people when you walk in each day.** At lunch or breaks, make small talk, such as about the weather or sports, or simply say "How's it going?" when you see them in the hallways at work.

- **Dress and groom for the part.** This includes wearing matching clothing and washing and styling hair. These are signs that you are professional, and this behavior makes others more comfortable around you. Observe how others look to get a feel for the culture.

Disclosing Your Diagnosis

Deciding whether to disclose that you have Asperger's can be tricky. The Americans with Disabilities Act (ADA) offers reasonable accommodations for people to do their jobs (e.g., ergonomic desks or wheelchair-size spaces), but it does not provide services to help adults get their jobs done. Do not make the mistake of assuming that if you reveal you have Asperger's, you will automatically be legally protected by the ADA. You may even want to consult an employment lawyer before revealing that you have Asperger's to make sure you are proceeding in a way that will help and protect you.

You may be able to ask for what you need without stating that you have Asperger's. Consider your job. Is it conducive to remote work (or a private office)? If in doubt, talk to a friend about the feasibility of working from home before announcing your desire to your supervisor. Maybe working from home two days a week is a possibility worth mentioning. You can approach it like this: "I find that I am much more productive working at home, and I'm comfortable with the technology to do so." Try to use positive terms and highlight what these accommodations will allow you to do, instead of concentrating on your limitations (try to avoid saying, "I'm really freaked out by all the noise in this office. I need to work at home!") Frame your request in ways that show you are considering how to benefit your employer, such as how telecommuting will improve your productivity and strengthen your commitment to the company.

As challenging as it may be, much of getting what you need at work relies on your ability to advocate for yourself. Asserting yourself may not be your best skill, but you will need to, at times, in order to be successful and make sure you get the tools you need to succeed. If you have a hard time speaking up for yourself, practice. Sit down and say a few sentences out loud about what you need. State it calmly and clearly, and when the time comes to ask a coworker or boss for something, you'll be prepared.

CHAPTER 3

A Home of Your Own

Finding a new place to live can be daunting, but it's one of the most rewarding things about becoming an adult. Picture your own private haven to get away from it all, a place designed just for you. You set the rules, invite whomever you want, eat what you want (and if once in a while that means cookies for dinner, who's to tell you otherwise). Having your own place is the trademark of adulthood and can provide you with a feeling of success and empowerment, when these days, a large majority of people with ASDs live at home with a family member or caretaker. For you, it's not just about rent and access to transportation; it's also about your needs—for some, it's being completely alone at the end of the day, while for others a good living situation means roommates and friends, but their own room with a door and four walls. And then there are concerns you may never have had to deal with, like negotiating with a landlord or dealing with difficult roommates. But for all the hard work, being on your own, if you can, is totally worth it.

Okay, those are some of the benefits. Now the logistics. It's not just about finding the right place to store your stuff and live. You will need to arm yourself with some domestic skills: cooking, cleaning, doing laundry, and taking care of yourself. You'll also have to navigate a variety of social situations, such as working with a real estate agent or landlord and potentially recruiting roommates, in order to find a place. If you live in a large city, you may be up against some stiff competition, as everyone else is looking for that perfect place with the perfect price tag, too.

Another point to consider: how involved and influential are your parents? Their involvement can serve as a helpful resource, but it can also be a bit of a hindrance, especially if you can honestly admit that they might do too much for you. If this is the case, your parents may be resistant to you taking on more independent responsibilities, like moving out. But they won't be around forever—a sobering thought, but a real one—so the more you can do for yourself, the better your life will be.

This is an area where you may need to advocate for yourself. The more capable you show them you are, the more reassurance you will provide them with (and the more likely they will be to help). It might be useful to sit down with them and say, "I appreciate everything you do for me. And I will always value your help. But I want to start doing more for myself, and this will be good for everyone." Encourage them to be a part of the transformation. If you don't cook for yourself, let them help you learn. Then take the reins and start making one meal a day—for the whole family. If you don't know how to run the washing machine, learn. The more you demonstrate you can do things for yourself, the more your parents will adjust to the idea—and wisdom—of you gaining your independence.

Jonathan's Story

Jonathan is a bright Aspie who did well in high school and was accepted into a computer science program at a state university about 100 miles away from where he grew up. While he certainly had the smarts to succeed in college, he wasn't ready for independent living. Once on campus, he usually slept through his alarm and rarely made it to class. He also couldn't manage long-term assignments, in part because he was not proactive in his learning and in part because he has coexisting ADHD and executive-function issues. As a result, he failed to plan ahead—missing the deadline for several key assignments—and did not study enough to pass his final exams in some subjects. Ultimately, he dropped out of college and returned to his parents' house. He finished his computer science program, graduating with high honors, and at 22 was still living with his parents. He accepted a well-paying position as a computer programmer at a medical device company.

Jonathan moved to a nearby apartment, but again he found himself unable to anticipate and handle all the demands of living on his own. His parents had not discussed the importance of budgets with him ahead of time, so while he had budgeted enough money for rent, he didn't consider or save for other expenses, including heat, water, electricity, cable TV, Internet service, and his cell phone. As a result, he constantly ran out of money before the end of the month. He allowed a childhood friend to move in with him, but to Jonathan's dismay, his new roommate was loud and disruptive and consistently late paying his share of the rent. It wasn't going well.

Jonathan spent most nights in his apartment alone playing video games because he wasn't sure how to connect with other adults. Most of his meals consisted of microwaved dinners because his cooking skills were nonexistent. To add to it all, his roommate continually got angry at Jonathan for not understanding his sarcasm was intended as a joke and for hanging around when he brought dates home. Jonathan found living with this roommate so stressful that he turned more and more inside himself until playing video games was the only thing he did besides going to work. After six months of living on his own, he decided to move back with his parents, where at least he would get a home-cooked meal and have enough money left over at the end of the month to spend on video games and his cell phone.

Jonathan's experience highlights some of the difficulties Aspies might face as they transition from living at home to living on their own. There is a lot to consider, but as the preceding story illustrates, there's also a whole lot you can do to plan ahead and prevent the pitfalls that Jonathan stumbled into, including educating yourself and working with a trusted friend or family member to consider all the necessary issues before moving out. From finding a suitable roommate and budgeting to cultivating friendships, read on for some ideas that will help you tackle each phase of the process.

//

Finding Home

Finding the right place to live can be confusing simply because it's a big world, and there is no one right answer. What might be best for others may not be right for you. The best way to find a comfortable place is to consider all the options. Here are the major variables that will guide your choice:

- Do you want to live in the city, suburbs, or a rural area?

- Depending on where you live, how will you get to work?

- How long will your commute take from that place? Are you okay with this?

- Do you want to be around stores and restaurants, or are you more interested in spending most of your time at home?

- What features are most important to you in a place to live (e.g., a private entrance, a private bathroom, a balcony, a lot of light)?

- What can you comfortably afford on your salary?

- How important are sensory issues to you? For example, do you need a very quiet location? If so, you may want to steer clear of large apartment buildings and busy streets.

- Do you have pets? If so, you need to ask whether they are allowed in the places you are considering renting.

Autism Speaks, an autism advocacy organization, has published a list of the best and worst places to live in the United States if you have autism. This list was based on a poll of people across the country, on variables such as access to resources and services, employer flexibility, access to medical care, and recreational opportunities. See the Resources section on page 107 for more details. If access to services is important to you, find out whether the area you are considering has these types of resources available.

Once you've sorted out what matters to you, you are ready to start looking. Keep an open mind; there may not be one ideal place, and it may be difficult to get the perfect place if you are on a tight budget. However, you can get a place that feels comfortable and that will allow you to rest and relax after a day in the office or out in the world.

Eyes Open: What to Look For

Okay, you've narrowed down your vision, and you're ready to check out some places. Now the fun begins. Checking out potential places to live as an adult can be a pretty empowering experience. This is *your* place—you call the shots, so choose wisely. First, contact the real estate agent or other representative to tour the places you are

BUDGET CONSIDERATIONS: DO THE MATH

Here are the expenses you may need to save money for each month:

- rent
- security deposit
- cable
- Internet
- electricity
- heat/gas/hot water
- car/gas/repairs/insurance
- commuting costs (bus fare, etc.)
- medical expenses (including dental, vision, psychiatric, and prescriptions)
- savings/nest egg/ emergency
- spending money (hobbies, clothing, social, holidays)

interested in seeing. It's important that you get out and see the apartments. Don't just rely on pictures on the Internet, which can make a place look deceptively large or nicer than it really is. If you are using a real estate agent, ask if they charge a fee or commission. And don't be tempted to rent the first place you see. The more places you look at, the better idea you will get of all the different kinds of properties out there. Next, invite a trusted friend or family member to join you on these visits to get a second opinion.

Once you've set some appointments, spend a little time sitting in these potential places. If you are working with a real estate agent, ask to sit in the place and monitor the noise level, light, and so on. Keep in mind that some places can be quiet during the day but might be louder during the morning or evening commute or at night. You can always do a drive-by at different times of the day to get a feel for

STARTING SMALL: RENTING A ROOM

Renting a room is a popular alternative, especially for those just starting out who may not be able to afford an apartment. Rooms can often be rented on a month-by-month basis, which can be a preferable option for people new to the yearlong lease contract that many apartments require. Many room rentals include a private bedroom and bathroom, though others have shared bathrooms, and then you share the common areas with others to some degree. How much you share depends on if it's a shared living arrangement with other renters or if it's somebody's home. If it's the latter, you might just get a shelf in the refrigerator. Many postings, such as those on Craigslist, contain information about fellow renters (e.g., "We are all students," "We host crazy parties all weekend long," "We are professionals, and we enjoy a quiet home") that can be helpful in determining a good fit.

the noise level or overall vibe. If you are sensitive to light, consider what the lighting is like in any house or apartment you look at. Keep in mind that you can make changes to most places, even if they are rentals, such as putting up blinds, changing the lighting, painting the walls, and of course bringing in your own furniture and belongings. However, if the atmosphere of the place makes you feel anxious or uncomfortable for any reason—the level of noise inside the building or outside, lighting, smells, or layout—you will likely not be comfortable there. Continue your search to find a place where you will feel rested and calm. If you are working and dealing with the sensory and emotional demands of an office or workspace all day, it's critical to find sanctuary in a place where you feel totally at peace.

Some adults with Asperger's have therapy dogs that help them by soothing their anxiety and helping them meet other people. Being in the company of a dog can be a wonderful way to meet other people and help you feel less isolated. If you go out with your dog, people will be drawn to your pet and ask you questions about him or her. Your pet will also make you feel more comfortable with other people. There are expenses involved in feeding and taking care of a dog, however, so remember to factor that into your monthly budget. In addition, you will have to make sure that the place you choose is right for you and your pet.

Working with Your Landlord

It's wise to have your landlord on your good side, in the event of issues like a leaking sink or toilet, a door that doesn't lock, window shades that don't work, or a noisy neighbor. Two things you can do to ensure good standing with the landlord are: pay your rent on time every month, and only contact the landlord during normal business hours, except during a true emergency (don't let that water pouring from a broken pipe wait until morning).

Getting what you need from your landlord is also an exercise in self-advocacy. Since you can't rely on your parents for this one, planning ahead will help. Practice stating clearly and calmly what you need before you ask your landlord. Then, when the time comes to make your request, you'll know exactly what to say. You can practice making these requests with a friend or mentor first, and you can rehearse responding to common ways in which the landlord might answer your request. All this practice may seem silly, but it aims to set you up for an effective and fruitful dialogue with your landlord, in order to get what you want.

SENSORY CONCERNS

Sensory issues can affect your living situation. For example, if there is too much noise in your building or neighborhood, you may find it difficult to rest, sleep, or relax. One solution is to invest in noise-cancelling headphones for the occasional loud party next door. However, if noise is continually an issue, you can politely ask your neighbors to quiet down. If that doesn't work, you might need to ask your landlord to get involved. The landlord can intervene and tell consistently noisy neighbors to quiet down. Getting enough sleep and battling insomnia can be real struggles for Aspies. It's important to set your place up in an optimal way to get the rest you need to function well the next day. Consider positioning your bed away from common walls, running a fan for "white noise," or any other strategies you may think of.

Other sensory issues can include overly harsh fluorescent lighting or other types of overhead lighting that seem too glaring. You can turn these off and instead use lamps. Perhaps the smell of a particular apartment or room bothers you. While you can use candles, incense, or air fresheners to get rid of temporary smells, make sure the apartment smells good before moving in. Odors that continually offend your senses can make your new place unpleasant and be tough to adapt to, so it's vital to sniff out these potentially off-putting smells.

Getting the Roommate Equation Right

There are some obvious positives to having a roommate. The biggest perk, of course, is that person can help you defray the cost of rent and other expenses, such as food. And even if you don't become best friends (most roommates have their own lives and friends), you can enjoy a respectful coexistence. A good roommate can help you feel less isolated. On the other hand, a roommate who is insensitive or annoying, or you simply don't get along with, can cause a lot of stress. Here are some common situations that can arise with roommates. Discuss them before moving in, and keep in mind some tricks for how to handle them:

- **Cleanliness:** You may have seen the classic movie and television show *The Odd Couple*, in which Felix Unger, a compulsive neatnik, rooms with Oscar Madison, a complete slob. Felix and Oscar's different attitudes toward cleanliness make them unlikely roommates. It's difficult to live with someone whose ideas of how to keep the place are so different from yours. When or before you begin rooming with someone, sit down to establish agreeable ground rules about how you will keep the place and who will clean. Work together to assign duties fairly; try to be open and flexible when you can, so you can be firm when you need to. Decide things like who will clean the bathroom each week and who will vacuum. It's a good idea to split these tasks so that you do them one week and your roommate does them the next.

- **Sharing:** Your roommate may want to share some of your possessions, such as your computer, books, or video game console. You may not want to share these belongings, so be sure to make that clear to your roommate before you start living together. By the same token, your roommate may want

INDEPENDENT LIVING PROGRAMS

These types of programs are an alternative to living on your own. Independent living programs for adults with Asperger's provide a bridge from living with your parents to living completely on your own. Many offer classes in job skills and life skills such as cooking, doing laundry, making a budget, socializing, and exercising. In some programs, adults first live in dormitories and then in semi-independent cottages or apartments where they are often visited by people who help them set up their lives in their own places.

to keep their belongings just for private use, so respect these boundaries. Be sure to ask before borrowing or using your roommate's belongings.

- **Food concerns:** If you have particular food needs and are sensitive to the taste and smell of foods that may impact your living together, explain this to your roommate beforehand. You may or may not choose to share food; work this out ahead of time, with a plan for how much each of you will contribute and how you'll divide the shopping duties. While some roommates share grocery shopping and cooking, you may not be able to do so if you have special requirements, or you may simply want to do your own thing.

- **Rent:** Before you decide to live with a roommate, make sure that person is responsible about money, and let them know when the rent is due. If your roommate does not pay the rent or utilities on time consistently, you might need to ask them to move out.

- **Having people over:** Set ground rules about when you can each have guests over—perhaps discuss hours, and definitely discuss overnights. If allowed and okay with both of you, how often is it acceptable? Anybody who is going to stay over night after night should be contributing to the rent! If you and your roommate cannot agree, or if your roommate doesn't abide by your agreement, you may need to call it quits.

- **Pets:** You and your roommate should agree in advance on whether you'll be cohabitating with pets. If so, you should talk about whether the pets are yours, theirs, or ours. In other words, who will take responsibility for the dog, cat, or snake? Or will you work together? Many Aspies are very attached to their pets and may not welcome another person's supervision of their animal. If you feel this way, you need to make that clear by saying something like, "You can pet him and give him these treats, but I would prefer to take care of him."

- **Communication:** Your roommate should be someone you can talk to, at least on a basic level. For example, you may need to tell this person that you have Asperger's, or you may simply need to tell your roommate what makes you comfortable or uncomfortable without revealing you have Asperger's. Whether or not you reveal your Asperger's, they should be understanding and approachable. Even if the person isn't your best friend,

You may want to ask the landlord if you can pay your portion of the rent separately from your roommate. Avoid handing money to your roommate unless you know and trust that person implicitly. Dividing up the utility bills is also a good idea. Perhaps offer to take responsibility for the electric bill, and let your roomie handle the cable and Internet. Asking to take care of the critical utilities—the ones you can't live without—will enable you to be in control of the important things. Sharing the utilities also gives you some leverage. If your roomie fails to give you money for the electric bill, don't give your roomie money for the cable and Internet!

Even if you consider your roommate a friend, there are definitely times to give them some space. If your room-mate has a steady partner, you shouldn't have to run into the bedroom and close the door every time that person comes. But you don't want to plop yourself on the couch next to them every time they watch a Friday evening flick together. Instead, say hi with a smile, then go read a book, go for a walk, or make other plans.

they should be a friend. After all, one of the reasons to live with a roommate is to have someone to hang out with. That doesn't mean that you should do everything together or that you can't have other friends; in fact, there are times that you should give your roommate space. But you should enjoy that person's company and be certain you can get along with in a respectful way.

Chat Notes: Negotiating with Landlords and Roommates

Here are some common scenarios that you may face with your landlord or roommate, and some ideas for scripts you can use in these situations.

Common Scripts for Your Landlord

You: *"I am sorry to bother you, but there is a problem with my _____ (fill in the problem, such as sink, toilet, shower, or stove). Is there a time you can fix it?"*

If your landlord is not willing to offer help, you can use the following script:

> **You:** *"I've asked you several times to fix my stove. It's been three days since I last asked you to fix it. If you don't repair it within the next few days, I'm going to have to hold back some of the rent until the repairs are made. When you make the repairs, I will pay the rent."*

It's important to document any issues that you have with your apartment, including the date the issue started and the dates on which you asked the landlord for repairs. If possible, put your complaints in writing, in an e-mail or note. Also, take pictures of what has fallen into disrepair. While communicating with your landlord, stay calm. You can maintain a civil relationship with your landlord even when you are disagreeing. Think of it as business, not personal. Remember that you have resources and rights, and you don't need to get angry to get results.

Common Scripts for Your Roommate

> **You:** *"The _____ (fill in the issue) is really getting bad, and the schedule says it's your turn to clean it. When can you get to this?"*

If your roommate consistently does not respond, you can say something like:

> **You:** *"Before you moved in, we decided on a schedule. You would _____ (fill in the task, such as cleaning the bathroom) every other week, and I would do it the other week. It's pretty bad in there. If you can't do it, I'm going to have to ask you to pay more rent so we can hire a cleaning person."*

Try to remain calm during these conversations, and remember that you're responding to someone who is being lazy or thoughtless, not hostile. If your roommate is not fulfilling their responsibilities, you may have to ask that person to move out.

Here is another script you might use if your roommate is inconsiderate:

You: *"Before you moved in, we agreed that we'd ask friends to leave by 11 on weeknights so the other person could get some sleep. I just wanted to give you a heads up, this is becoming an issue for me. Is it possible for you to ask your friends to leave by this time?"*

If your roommate is unable or unwilling to enforce these rules, you may have to ask that person to move out.

The Basics

Once you are living in your own place, you'll want to make a budget of all your monthly expenses, including rent, heat, gas, cable, cell phone, Internet, and transportation. See how much money is left over and use your discretionary cash wisely. If you don't already have one, set up a savings account for large upcoming expenses, such as trips, large purchases, or unexpected issues (like car repairs). If you need therapy or other types of assistance, set aside money so you can access the services you need.

You should also set up a schedule to keep track of when to pay certain expenses. Most banks offer online bill payment, making it fairly easy and efficient to pay bills without sending checks through the mail. This type of system might be easy for you to maintain. Many banks offer automatic payments, deducted each month from your account. Otherwise, you will need to note on your calendar or in your phone when bills are due to remind you to pay them on time. If you are late paying bills, your credit score may go down. This is an important score for your independence. It helps banks and other institutions decide whether to give you loans, lease you a car, and so on, as well as what interest rate to charge you. So you want to do your best to pay bills on time on a regular basis.

You may not need one, but you can also make a schedule for cleaning your place (including taking out the garbage, cleaning the kitchen and bathroom, vacuuming, and changing your bed linen) and doing your laundry. If you have a laundry room in your building, you're lucky. If not, you will need to find a nearby Laundromat and schedule time to go there.

You will also need to find a nearby grocery store and make a list of the items you need each week, then go purchase, prepare, and eat them. *Sounds tiring, all this work for a simple peanut butter sandwich.* Seriously, making simple foods at home can save you money, make you feel healthier, and increase your self-confidence. Won't it be fun to say, "I am an excellent cook." But getting started, many Aspies struggle to find their food groove—a diet that is healthy and that involves a variety of foods they like. As you start living on your own and cooking for yourself, take a chance and try some new foods—the ones that intrigue you, not the ones your mom always said you should like. Start slowly by introducing one new food into your diet as you feel ready. If the texture of food presents an issue for you, try blended foods or smoothies that might be easier for you to taste and digest. If you find it difficult to make your own food, check out CookingWithAutism.com/cookbook. The organization at this site published a cookbook with recipes that have been vetted by people with autism who have found them easy to follow. The cookbook also emphasizes the importance of making and eating food with other people for relaxation and enjoyment.

Streamline bill paying. Call the companies you will pay each month and ask them if you can pay their bill the first of the month (or any day that works for you). If you can arrange a set date with all these companies, you can simply make it a point to sit down on the same day each month and pay all bills at once, so nothing slips through the cracks.

MAKE YOUR PLACE YOUR OWN

When you step into a new apartment, it may not look like where you imagined you would live. But there are small, easy steps you can take to personalize your space and make it comfortable—even awesome—to you. Look online, order catalogs, watch HGTV, and wander around stores. Visit vintage stores if you prefer secondhand furniture in retro styles, and look for textiles, pillows, and other objects that appeal to your senses. Consider the smells that you want to introduce with candles or sprays. These steps will help you learn about your style and make your space your own.

Disclosing Your Diagnosis

Carefully consider whether you want to disclose that you have Asperger's to your roommate, landlord, and other people you live with or near. You may need to disclose your needs to your roommate before living with that person, including your need for quiet or the way in which you feel comfortable keeping the apartment—however, simply explaining your needs in a straightforward way may be sufficient. Similarly, it may not be necessary to disclose to your landlord that you have Asperger's. Keep in mind that unfortunately, not everyone in the neurotypical world is knowledgeable about what being an Aspie means, so they may judge you unfairly or make presuppositions about you that aren't true. Don't be afraid to answer their questions; you can educate others in a way that you know is accurate. Again, it may be enough to simply explain your needs to your landlord, such as keeping your space quiet, without revealing that you have Asperger's.

Sometimes it seems easier to have a hard-and-fast rule about whether to disclose that you have Asperger's. But as an adult, it might be better to decide on a case-by-case basis. For example, if you become friends with your roommate and think that person is trustworthy, you can tell them. However, if you have a more distant relationship or one that is not as trusting, it may not be necessary to do so, and you may not want to. In addition, it may be necessary to disclose to your roommate that you have Asperger's if your needs seem odd or extreme to this person, even if they seem routine and acceptable to you. For example, some Aspies have a strong reaction to certain types of foods and smells, which means that you cannot cook or eat with your roommate. It may just be easier to explain why you have these needs, otherwise your roommate might assume you are just being difficult.

CHAPTER 4

Romance, Anyone?

When living on your own, you may find companionship and fun by pairing up with a romantic partner or just going out on some dates. A romantic partner can really transform your world: Not only can they help you feel less isolated and more connected, they can help make life more fun than you imagined, too. Dating and finding a romantic partner may have been difficult in the past, and having Asperger's can make these situations more complicated. However, there are strategies to help you navigate these confusing waters. For starters, there are common ways that people expect you to act in dating situations, and by understanding what they are, you can start on the right track and modify them to your liking as you go.

Philip's Story

When Philip was in college, he spent most of his time in his dorm room playing video games. There was a cute girl in his history class he wanted to ask out on a date, but he didn't know how. He spent a lot of time thinking about asking her out, but he found he couldn't. Instead, he looked for dates on an online site, and he starting chatting with a girl who seemed to share his interests, including gaming and medieval history. After a month of chatting, they decided to meet at a local coffee shop. When Philip met his date, he was disappointed. She looked and seemed different than she had online, and she talked too much for his liking. At the end of the date, he was walking away from her building when she put her arms around him and started kissing him. He kissed her back without really wanting to, and then she gave him her number. He put the number on his desk, but it sat there for months until he threw it away. She tried to chat with him online, but he did not respond.

Philip idealized his date before meeting her, and then he was disappointed when the reality did not match up to what he thought she had presented online. While he found someone he wanted to ask out in his class, he was too shy to do so. As a result, he wound up going out with a woman he wasn't particularly interested in, and he didn't understand the signals she was sending him at the end of the date. There is a common script to many types of dates that includes speaking before the date, meeting at a restaurant or other public place to talk more, and then possibly having some type of physical contact at the end of the date, even just a hug or a kiss on the cheek. Philip wanted to have contact with women, but he did not feel comfortable with this type of planned script, and you may not either. This chapter presents some ideas about how you can find a romantic partner by following a script that feels more comfortable to you.

//

Getting Your Feet Wet

Many Aspies can tell you about disastrous dating situations. In fact, most neurotypical people have a hard time when they start to date, too. These types of situations can make you wary or even opposed to trying to date again. With a bit of guidance, however, you might find the dating scene more to your liking. It really can be fun—especially when you find the right person.

To get your feet wet, begin with simple dates and meet-ups. For example, if you are already acquainted with someone you met in your building or in a group, ask that person if they want to grab a coffee. Don't think of it as a date. Think of it as having coffee with a friend. Start with some steps like this and consider joining an adult Asperger's support group (see the Resources section on page 107 for more information). Keep in mind that the person you meet doesn't need to be the perfect date or the love of your life. Instead, use the experience as a way to take a small risk without putting too much on the line and to practice making conversation and connections.

You might also consider seeking out an informal mentor. That person might be a friend, acquaintance, or family connection who is willing to hear about your experiences and offer you suggestions in a nonjudgmental way. You can ask a parent, but that might be awkward. Instead, try to find another adult who is less likely to react defensively or protectively to what you say. In other words, your parents might be too willing to defend you, or they might be too ready to criticize you. An adult who is more likely to be impartial and ready to listen makes a better social mentor.

Many Aspies enjoy dating other Aspies, because they bring companionship and understanding along with similar needs and interests. Other Aspies like the balance of dating someone with a neurotypical profile who can provide another point of view and offer interests and talents that may be different than their own. Some Aspies prefer to get to know people online, while others prefer meeting romantic partners in person or through groups. You can try out various methods before deciding which way is most comfortable for you. There is no one right way to find a partner—people find partners in all kinds of unlikely places.

Dating 101

This book is not intended to be an all-around guide to dating, but it can point you to some of the promises and pitfalls of dating as an Aspie. Everyone is different, but there are some general Aspie behaviors that warrant consideration when you're starting to date. Keep in mind that many neurotypicals have a common and timeworn storyline in their heads when they go on a date. This storyline doesn't always work and is in part borrowed from Hollywood romantic comedies. While it isn't strictly necessary to follow this storyline, you should know in advance what it is so that if you don't follow along, you'll understand how you are going against dating conventions.

The narrative goes something like this: One person asks another out to a public place or to do an activity, usually a drink or a meal. They make conversation and get to know each other. After one of these dates, they may expect to have some type of physical contact along with a bit of implied seduction, meaning they don't dive right into physical contact, but make flirtatious conversation or movements first. It's a bit of a dance, and the multiple steps can be confusing. That's why it may be necessary at times to reveal that you are an Aspie or simply that you don't follow this storyline (more on this later in the chapter). First, here are some common dating scenarios and suggestions for how to respond to them. If you need extra practice or clarification about some of these situations, consult a mentor, a friendly adult who can help in a nonjudgmental way.

NOBODY'S PERFECT

Research by Asperger's experts such as Tony Attwood suggests that Aspie men and women differ in their dating behaviors. Aspie men tend to seek partners who compensate for their shortcomings or perceived shortcomings, such as their lack of social interest or inability to take care of routine household tasks. Aspie women, on the other hand, tend to look for romantic partners who are similar to themselves. Would you rather find someone who brings diverse interests and points of view, or would you feel more at home with someone who will understand your quirks, needs, and interests?

Some research suggests that Aspies may tend to look for an ideal partner—one who might be difficult to find in real life. If this is the case, you may find yourself continually disappointed with dates who seem to fall short in some way. Finding companionship is not always about finding perfection; you will be looking a long time! You can enjoy someone's company without their being perfect; in fact, quirks and idiosyncrasies can be quite endearing. The key is not to be overly critical when you are getting to know someone. Don't let small things get in the way of finding out if you enjoy being together. Once you get to know someone, these types of issues may not matter as much if you truly like their company.

Making Conversation

Some Aspies are talkative but may tend to get off the subject, while others struggle just to make light conversation. It can be hard for Aspies to respond appropriately to neurotypicals' conversational patterns. So how do you do it? Some good ways to start off a conversation on a date include speaking about a friend you have in common, asking your date about their job and hobbies, or asking what movies or books your date enjoys. When you find a common thread—*Hey, she likes anime, too*—you'll have opened a door to a common interest. Avoid speaking too long about a topic that may not interest your date. For example, if you bring up subway lines and your date isn't interested in this topic—which you may be able to tell because your date doesn't respond, looks away, or (yikes) even yawns—change the subject by asking what he or she is interested in. Nothing interests people more than speaking about themselves, so this is a great way to get the conversational ball rolling, and keep it going with follow-up questions such as "Can you tell me more about that?" or "I didn't know that! Why do you think that is?" People are usually quite talkative when speaking about themselves.

If making conversation is difficult for you, try a dating activity that offers a diversion or that reduces the need for conversation: a movie, a hike, mini-golf, or bowling—may make it unnecessary to talk the entire time. These activities will also provide you with some conversational focus: "Wow, are you in a league or something?" or "Look at that bird over there. What do you think it is?" Try to mix it up by asking questions and sharing a bit about yourself in the process: "Oh, you like to cook? Do you prefer cooking or baking? What are your favorite dishes? I am a master at making French toast, but that's about it!" Don't dominate the conversation. You may get really excited about certain things, but conversations need to flow, and your date should feel like you care about what he or she has to say. If you feel like the date isn't going well, it's fine to end it in a polite manner and go your separate ways.

ONLINE DATING

Some Aspies find it easier to start dating using online dating sites. Online dating can be a relatively nonconfrontational and painless way to meet someone who shares your interests and to chat before you meet—either by phone or electronically—to make sure there is a good fit.

Online dating can have drawbacks, however. There's the "I love long walks on the beach" theory, which suggests guys pretend to be romantic fools in order to attract people. And women have their own lines, too. Yes, people can present themselves in ways that, while not entirely false, represent only part of the reality. (Others completely misrepresent themselves.)

Also, some people, Aspies included, get too comfortable in the getting-to-know-you-online phase and never try to meet people in person. While dating online is fine, it's generally just a first step. You can enjoy much more companionship and physical contact and limit your social isolation if you try to eventually meet dates in person.

And try to keep it real. You can get caught up in situations where you are pursuing someone who isn't interested in you, or in which you are just spinning your wheels—e-mailing or chatting without moving the relationship forward. You may also find yourself pursuing people who are unlikely partners and don't share your interests or needs, just because they wrote back. For these reasons, you should also try to meet people in your social circle—in groups or clubs you may belong to. That way, you will be likely to find someone who shares your interests, someone you know you will get along with before you go on a date.

Let's also address stimming, or those comforting, repetitive behaviors such as rocking, clapping, snapping, or tapping that you may have used to soothe yourself since you were little. Stimming in private is fine and natural, but try to avoid it on the first date, even if you're super nervous. If you must, maybe go with something discreet like rubbing your fingers together under the table. If being able to stim around your romantic partner is important to you, you may need to disclose that you have Asperger's.

Looking Good and Feeling Good

Aspies tend to dress for comfort rather than style. While it's great to choose styles and fabrics that make you feel good and keep your senses happy, there are times when you want to look good, and a date is definitely one of those times. If you are struggling to find the right clothes for a date, ask a stylish friend. You can shop in a vintage or secondhand store if you need to keep it cheap.

When you're getting ready to go out on a date, groom yourself appropriately. Shower, shave if necessary, and wear clean clothes. Choose clothes that make you feel comfortable but that also allow you to feel confident. Many Aspie women have spent a lifetime being told they aren't following traditional gender and social roles because they refuse to follow fashion and, in some cases, groom their hair. Some wear their hair over their face or in their eyes to avoid looking at others and being looked at too closely. This is understandable, but it might be helpful to carry out some simple grooming extras when you start dating. That doesn't mean you have to change yourself entirely, but it does mean you should present everything that's special about you in the best light. Take some time to find a hairstyle and outfit that presents you in a flattering way, and if you need help, ask a stylish and trusted friend, your hairdresser, the salesperson in a store whose look you like, or the person behind the makeup counter at the department store. You can even explain that you prefer a certain look; your hairdresser may know just the style to complement both your features and your preference.

Being Cool

When Aspies are interested in someone, they can tend to go a bit overboard—for example, calling or texting that person 15 times in a day (which is going overboard, unless the other person is doing it too). While there is absolutely nothing wrong with expressing interest, keep it within a reasonable range, even if you're dying to get in touch with that person. What seems like normal behavior to an Aspie can seem like overkill or even stalking to a neurotypical person. You may think that such behavior seems charming or expresses interest, but most neurotypicals prefer taking things slow and not overdoing it. Of course, if you are really interested in someone, there is no reason you can't make a nice gesture at a special time, such as an anniversary or birthday. However, try to keep it appropriate to your relationship's current level. Carrying out grand gestures such as showering your romantic interest with flowers, gifts, messages, phone calls, or texts before you are pretty serious may scare the person off.

Social media can be really tricky in this regard. Don't be tempted to use it to track every move your romantic interest makes or to read or respond to their every post on Facebook. Social media allows you to get far too involved in the lives of people you've just met, but the intimacy you may feel with them by tracking their movements is not true intimacy, and it's definitely not an invitation to get involved in their personal business. It takes time to develop the type of relationship in which it's truly okay to become active participants on the other's social media. Take your time, and when it comes to social media, let them make the first move. If they "friend" you or begin responding to your posts, you can take this as a go-ahead to respond to some of theirs. Again, play it cool. Overwhelming the person with communication or becoming obsessed with their movements is not healthy or helpful.

If you are truly interested in the person, a better way to get to know them is to listen to what they say, convey interest in their thoughts and feelings, and be responsive. Showering them with grand gestures is not necessary or realistic at the beginning of a relationship. But with time, you may get your chance.

DECIPHERING SOCIAL SIGNALS

It can be hard to recognize another person's signals and figure out what they mean. Here are some common signals and body language and clues about what they might mean:

- **Your date touches your arm, shoulder, leg, or hand.** These are clues the person is interested in you. In other words, they are forms of flirting and conveying the person is interested in having physical contact. One caveat: some people are comfortable putting their hands on people's shoulders, so this may not be a clue in and of itself. However, for most people, this behavior is a sign that they are interested.

- **Your date touches their hair or flips it (particularly a woman).** This may also be a sign of interest or flirtation, especially if it happens again and again. One little movement of the hair out of the eyes doesn't mean anything. But repeatedly flipping the back of the hair—that probably means something good.

- **Your date sits close to you.** This is also potentially a sign of interest and flirtation. Other potential expressions of interest include laughing, looking up at you from lowered eyes, and looking into your eyes.

- **Your date moves away.** The person may be reacting to something you said or could be trying to create some distance from you. Other behaviors that may be intended to show disinterest are yawning, foot tapping (unless it's another Aspie), looking away, or repeatedly looking at one's watch or phone.

If you are on a date, check in on your own body language, too. If you want to convey interest, try looking your date in the eye, even if just momentarily or occasionally. While this behavior may seem strange or uncomfortable for you, looking for even a few seconds is pretty important, and will help convey to your date that you're interested and paying attention.

Finding Intimacy That Fits

Some Aspies want to get physical with others, while others aren't interested in physical contact and sex. Others want sex but not a lot of nonsexual physical contact. The script for a neurotypical date can, but doesn't always, end with some degree of physical contact or sex. Be aware that if the date concludes and is going well, your date might expect a kiss, a hug, or more physical contact. If you don't feel comfortable going this route, it's okay. But you might need to be straightforward with your date and explain that you don't really feel comfortable with physical contact. You might emphasize that it has to do with your needs and that it isn't a reaction to your date—"It's not you, it's me"—because that person might feel bad if they think it's because you don't find them attractive or desirable.

If you want to be physical in a way that involves sex but little nonsexual physical contact (because touch makes you feel uncomfortable and vulnerable) you need to explain your needs to your date. Many neurotypicals expect a long process of seduction, including hugging, kissing, and other physical contact before initiating sex. While there is no one right way to be intimate with someone, your date should know in advance if you can't carry out this process of physical contact. In this case, you may need to disclose to your partner that you have Asperger's.

You might need to use a script like the following (feel free to change or adapt it to your needs): "I really like you, and I think you like me, too. Please let me know if I'm wrong. I also don't want to presume too much, but I'd like to have more physical contact with you. Would that be all right with you?" If the other person responds, yes, then continue. "I like you and am attracted to you, but sometimes touching makes me uncomfortable, so I like to be intimate without a lot of additional physical contact. If this is okay with you, I can let you know what I mean."

It can be awkward to bring up issues like this at first, but this type of conversation will serve as a good measure of whether your partner is interested enough in you to consider doing what makes you feel comfortable. If the other person disagrees, this may be a sign that getting involved with that person in an intimate way may not work.

Breaking Up Is Hard to Do

You will inevitably experience a breakup. We all do. This happens, of course, because you end it or because the other person does. Either way, it hurts. If you need to break up with someone, do it honestly, thoughtfully, and cleanly. If you know you don't want to date that person again, don't leave open the possibility of restarting your relationship, and don't use the old line, "I'd like to stay friends," unless you really mean it. Instead, you can say something like the following:

> *"I've really enjoyed getting to know you the past few weeks, and I think you're great. But for my own purposes, I think I need to move on and date other people. I'm sorry about this, and I hope there are no hard feelings."*

You may have to accept that the other person will react with disbelief, surprise, or anger, and it's best to respond to these feelings in a calm way.

If the other person breaks up with you, even if you feel absolutely devastated, there isn't much you can do about it. Resist plaguing the other person with calls, texts, or e-mails begging them to get back together. These ploys don't work, and all they usually do is make the other person happier they broke it off with you and make you feel miserable. Instead, try to immerse yourself in an activity you enjoy (video games might help distract you, but you don't want to totally immerse yourself in the virtual world), and when you're ready, try to get back out there and find someone new to date through an online dating site, a social group, or friends.

ASPIE WOMEN

If you are an Aspie woman, you may have felt left out of or confused about social circles or dating, and you may have been taunted or bullied by others who didn't understand your specific ways. Though you're old enough now to realize that the bullies of your childhood were cruel and dysfunctional, what you suffered in the past is not always easily forgotten.

To find a place in the adult social world, you might decide to employ imitation and people-pleasing strategies to mask your confusion about social norms and your raw vulnerability. That is, trying to imitate friends or people you see on TV to feel more confident in social situations. Some of this role playing can be helpful, but it can also make you seem inauthentic and may not actually increase your confidence. After all, you're not really being yourself. You want to get to a point where you feel comfortable being *you*—especially in a romantic situation.

Aspie women are often, unfortunately, susceptible to abuse and dating inappropriate men because you crave flattery, which perhaps you haven't gotten enough of. You may also see yourself as socially immature, and if you haven't had a whole lot of positive social experiences, this may be an accurate assessment. As a result, you might choose romantic partners who are cruel and wrong for you, and you may feel unable to stand up for yourself in abusive or harmful situations.

To find someone who truly cherishes you for who you are, work on being yourself. There is no need to playact or turn yourself inside out trying to please others. Instead, start by deepening a friendship with someone you like and see if it becomes romantic. That way, you'll be dating someone who is friendly and unlikely to be harmful or abusive. Learn to say no to people who hurt you, and ask a friend to help you recognize potential partners who are promising and those who might be trouble.

Disclosing Your Diagnosis

It's generally a good idea to disclose you have Asperger's when you're dating someone. While you don't have to do so on the first date, it's best to let the person know sooner rather than later. This way, you'll be fair and genuine to the other person; you'll also get an idea of how open and accepting the other person is. If the other person is not accepting or understanding, it's probably a good sign this individual isn't right for you anyway.

You'll also want to disclose that you have Asperger's, and what your related needs are, before you are intimate. That way, when issues come up, the other person will know what to expect and won't be surprised or hurt in any way. It may take some time for the other person, if they are neurotypical, to understand your needs, but as long as they're trying, it's a good sign!

CHAPTER 5

The Social Scene

Now that you're on your own and working, you may feel tempted to spend every night on the sofa in your apartment reading or playing video games. *But that's where I'm comfortable!* Many Aspies feel they don't need many friends, or have one best friend, usually their partner or spouse, and that's fine. It may feel overwhelming to invest in many relationships or have to deal with the emotional input of lots of people, particularly after a long day's work. However, if you agree that you need to get out more, don't have a partner right now, or are feeling isolated, there are some low-impact ways you can meet people you like and reduce your sense of isolation.

We Know You'd Rather Not

Growing up, you may have found socializing difficult, problematic, even painful. You may have found yourself surrounded by people who didn't quite get you or who considered your compelling interests odd and quirky. You may also have found it difficult to follow social cues or follow the discussion in a group of people. At worst, you may have been plagued by bullies who abused you emotionally, physically, or both.

As a result, you may not have a warm association with social interactions, and prefer to stick to yourself. At the end of the day, after many hours of interacting with other people, most of us likely want nothing more than to hunker down at home and do whatever makes us happy, whether it's binge-watching our favorite show, reading, or gaming with virtual friends. Many neurotypicals also prefer solitude and peace, and others prefer a mix of socializing and solitude. Find the mix that works for you—but a mix of any kind is good. After all, there's a balance between being a total hermit and a social butterfly.

When you were a kid, you might have found out—the hard way—that your sense of humor was different from others'. You didn't get their jokes, and they didn't get yours. That's okay, and much of that experience is behind you now. You can connect with people who share your interests and your particular brand of humor. In the process, you'll start accepting the great parts of your personality and perhaps leave behind what you don't like. Socializing as an adult is not likely to replicate your childhood experiences. Instead, it can be a time to connect with and get to know people whose company you truly enjoy—and who enjoy yours.

Gaming: How Much Is Too Much?

Many Aspies enjoy gaming, and there are good reasons why. Gaming sets up a predictable, enjoyable universe for many people on the spectrum, in which you can rack up points, quantify your success, and understand the parameters and rules of the game. Many games, it would seem, are made by Aspies for Aspies. However, like all good things, too much gaming can spiral into an addiction. If you are gaming to the point that you're losing track of time and excluding everything else, you may actually be addicted. Gaming can get in the way of socializing, dating, and even working. Here are some signs you might be addicted to gaming:

- Nothing else has meaning or interest to you. Only gaming makes you happy.

- You're depressed or anxious when you're not gaming.

- When you're not gaming, you're often thinking about it.

- You are neglecting socializing and making friends.

- You are neglecting showering, sleeping, and eating.

If you're exhibiting any of those signs and think you have an addiction to gaming, there are gaming self-help programs for finding a satisfactory balance.

Where and How to Meet People

At this stage of your life, finding a place to work and live are probably your top priorities. You may even be looking for a person to settle down with. However, if you'd like to be more social, where can you start, especially if you're new to a city, town, or neighborhood?

- **At the office:** Work is a good place to meet friends, though keep in mind that it may not be the best place to find a date. Many officemates go out to bars or restaurants after work, particularly on Thursdays or Fridays. If this isn't your scene, there may also be work-related sports teams you'd like to join. These teams tend to be more about fun than about serious competition. You can even go just to cheer the players on.

- **Asperger's support groups:** Check out the Resources section on page 107 for some ideas about how to meet up with other Aspies in adult support groups. These are an invaluable resource—groups designed to bring together and support people who have many of the same issues and interests as you. Aside from the obvious social benefits of a group like this, some offer classes on how to cook, clean, and carry out other skills necessary for independent living, and others stage events where adults can get to know each other through fun activities.

- **Community or religious groups:** Even if you don't consider yourself religious, there are a growing number of faith-based organizations that offer a spectrum of social opportunities. Go online to see what's available. Your local church, temple, synagogue, or mosque probably runs ongoing service projects where people work together to help others. Many offer specific groups for young adults that involve socializing in a relaxed environment.

- **Groups involving an interest:** If you are interested in gaming, hiking, reading, sports, learning a language, tech—whatever, then find a group by looking for ads in your local coffee shop, community college, or newspaper, or by searching online using Eventbrite or Meet Up (MeetUp.com). Specialized groups offer connections to like-minded individuals who share your interests. Open your mind to new possibilities, too. By expanding your interests and trying something new, you may meet new

GO SLOW . . .

Socializing is a lot like dating; it takes time to develop deep and meaningful relationships that offer a lot of support and mutual help. Don't assume someone you've spent a few hours with is automatically your best friend, ready to drop everything to help you or happy to spend all his or her free time with you. It's good to go slowly with friendships and enjoy them as they develop. Realize that forming solid friendships takes time.

people and discover an activity that you enjoy and that helps you broaden your interests. That doesn't mean you should join a football team if you hate football. But you might enjoy hiking with others if you've always hiked on your own.

- **The dog park:** If you are a dog owner, walking your dog or visiting the dog park is the perfect way to meet other people who love dogs. You'll have a common interest that will allow you to spend time together. And if conversation doesn't come easy, dogs offer a nice diversion.

RECIPROCITY: THE IMPORTANCE OF GIVE-AND-TAKE

It's critical to realize that friendships and relationships, and even conversations with acquaintances, are dependent on give-and-take. If someone says "How are you?" the appropriate response isn't "Good." It's "I'm good. How are you doing?" Though this book emphasizes how people can help us, we must remember that to make and keep friends, it's equally important to give support back—to be a caregiver rather than just be cared for. Watch for opportunities to help that colleague, friend, or romantic interest—something like, "Hey, I can help with that; I know PowerPoint." Or "Wow, sounds like you had a rough day." If conversation's not your strong suit, try being noncommittally supportive by nodding your head or by shaking it in disbelief, or by simply saying, "I get what you mean."

REASONS TO SOCIALIZE

Even though you may prefer to spend a great deal of time in solitude, there are some compelling reasons to get out there and socialize:

- **Socializing with friends can help you meet that special someone who might become your romantic partner.** Friends can introduce you to people who may be right for you, and if there is a person who seems to spend a lot of time speaking with you at social gatherings, you may want to ask that person out on a date to see if the relationship could become something more.

- **Socializing with like-minded people helps you feel less lonely.** You may feel very isolated spending all your free time at home, and not even realize it. Socializing is a way to share your concerns, get (and give) some good advice, and make friends.

- **Socializing is a way to talk about shared interests.** You can join activities in which you are more likely to meet people who like the same things you do.

- **Socializing helps you network and hear about new groups, clubs, or even job opportunities.** While you don't want to spend every social occasion asking about job openings, you may hear of one while speaking with others, particularly if you let them know you are looking for a position.

- **Socializing helps you understand—and get better at—the rules of the neurotypical world.** While you may not want to replicate all these behaviors, it can help to understand them and see people using them. For example, by socializing, you can watch and learn how people make small talk, which can help you integrate with others on dates or in the office.

Friendly Activities

Just like dating, friendships can get off to a rocky start if you're doing something you don't like. Instead, start by socializing with people while doing an activity you enjoy. That way, you'll not only have built-in material for conversation with others, but you'll also likely find people you enjoy being with who apparently like the same activity. If you like gaming, you might enjoy playing with others online, but you can also play games with others in person. What a concept! Other activities you might try include running, hiking, rock climbing, photography, dog walking, or drawing. These are activities you can do by yourself, but why not share them with others? These types of activities don't require you to stay in lockstep with others, but you can do them in your own way while enjoying the companionship. Activities also allow you easy access to an area of conversation, as you can comment about what you're doing and ask your friends questions about their thoughts.

Disclosing Your Diagnosis

It may not be necessary to disclose that you are an Aspie to your friends, and certainly not to acquaintances whom you don't know very well. Though it may seem comforting to have an all-inclusive rule about whom you should tell, you may actually want to be a bit flexible in this regard and decide on a case-by-case basis. If you think a friend understands, that person might be a good person to tell, particularly if you've known him or her for a while or if you find you need to explain your needs. However, if you've just met someone, don't feel pressured to disclose. It's not as vital as sharing that information with, say, romantic partners, with whom your needs are much more critical and where it's important to speak about them in advance.

You can also share your needs and interests with friends without revealing that you have Asperger's, and you can even use your particular brand of humor. For example, you can say something along the lines of "Thanks for putting up with my habit of repeating things. I've been doing that since childhood. Have I told you I've been doing that since childhood?" It's not necessary to let the term Asperger's or the diagnosis define you. Instead, share what's unique about you with your friends without bringing up Asperger's, if it makes you feel more comfortable to do so. If you want to share your experience with Asperger's, though, it's totally your call.

CHAPTER 6

Taking Care of Yourself

Caring for yourself is critical to a successful and happy adult life. A good number of adult Aspies struggle with issues such as depression, anxiety, and insomnia. If you contend with these issues some or all of the time, you are not alone. But don't let it dictate your life. There is help out there, and, if you need it, do yourself a service and get it. In addition, some adult Aspies do not always eat a well-rounded diet. This can be due in part to issues around food and sensory problems. This chapter will help you consider ways to develop healthier habits and get the help you need to feel good in your skin.

Jess's Story

Jess considered herself pretty successful, as did her family. She struggled in elementary school with social problems and outbursts, but became a successful student in high school and went on to major in computer science at a prestigious college. She taught herself coding in middle school, so the academic part of college wasn't at all tough for her. In fact, she excelled at it, and found a high-paying job as a programmer at a software company right after graduation. The job seemed perfect for her: She could wear jeans and T-shirts and largely keep her own hours.

Jess moved into an apartment that her parents helped furnish, and she generally enjoyed spending time alone there. Her only relationship was a one-night affair in college that ended badly, and though she wanted to find a partner, she didn't do much about it. But things started to unravel a bit for Jess when she had to work on a cross-divisional team on a product that was of great importance to the company. When she expressed her dissatisfaction with her teammates' progress, they told her that she was unprofessional and reported her to the HR department. As a result, she was forced to take an anger management course, but she thought her outbursts were totally warranted because her teammates were too slow to keep up with her progress.

She began to feel tired all the time, in part because she suffered from insomnia and kept irregular hours, but it was getting worse. And while she'd always gotten by on her favorite diet of pizza and chips, she now felt sluggish. Her body ached, and worst of all, she started feeling an uncontrollable rage. She finally went to her general practitioner, who couldn't find anything wrong. But he did send Jess to a psychiatrist who, after speaking with Jess at length, diagnosed her with anxiety and depression. Jess was prescribed a common antidepressant and referred to a cognitive behavioral therapist. After about six weeks of therapy and medication, she began to feel better—less anxious, less angry, and less irritable. Her therapist helped her create strategies to deal with frustration with her colleagues, and she began to consider where her colleagues were coming from and how she might have made them feel. Within three months, she found that she felt much better and was even ready to start checking out some online dating sites.

In retrospect, Jess was fortunate that she saw her general practitioner, who picked up on her underlying anxiety and depression. Many mental illnesses go undiagnosed. Sometimes, anxiety and depression in adults can be hard to detect: It may manifest itself as anger or even physical pain, and there are many other ways it shows itself. If you suspect you have coexisting conditions along with Asperger's or have been feeling out of sorts, talk to your doctor and get the help you need to get your life back. This chapter will show you how to do so and acquaint you with some of the many types of help available to you.

//

Coexisting Conditions: The Plot Thickens

Not all Aspies have these conditions, but many adults with Asperger's or HFA may suffer from the following:

- **Sensory processing disorder:** Many adult Aspies recoil from sensations like touch or from certain noises or smells. You may also find that you have trouble handling the taste of certain foods and that you need motion or sensory input of different types to make yourself feel better physically and emotionally. While these types of symptoms are widely recognized in children with Asperger's, adults may also continue to struggle with them.

- **Sleep problems:** According to reputable studies, adults with Asperger's report a very high incidence of sleep problems.

These problems include insomnia and issues of falling asleep and staying asleep. Insomnia may result in the worsening of Asperger's symptoms and concurrent psychiatric conditions such as depression and anxiety.

- **ADD/ADHD and executive-function disorders:** Many adults with Asperger's struggle with issues related to attention, and they may also have a related but distinct condition called executive-function disorder, which results in difficulty organizing and planning, as well as trouble shifting from one activity to another.

- **Depression, anxiety, and other psychiatric conditions:** Research shows that people with Asperger's suffer from high rates of psychiatric disorders, including anxiety and depression. Scientists aren't sure whether these issues result from the isolation and difficulty that life with Asperger's can sometimes present, or whether these psychiatric issues are related to the hard wiring of Asperger's in the brain. Anxiety and depression can make adult Aspies more rigid and prone to emotional outbursts. Adult Aspies may also struggle with obsessive-compulsive disorder (OCD) or other ailments, and they may not always feel comfortable or adept at relaying their symptoms or struggles to doctors and mental health professionals.

Treatments for Coexisting Conditions

There are many treatments available for adults with Asperger's. To find the right person to help you, ask about their experience, including their background working with adults with Asperger's. Work with professionals who are informative, make you feel comfortable, and have experience helping adults with the same issues you are facing.

Therapies

- **Sensory integration therapy:** The goal of sensory integration therapy is to help the nervous system process sensory information in a more typical way. Sensory integration focuses on three systems: the vestibular system, which uses components of the inner ear to detect movements of the head; the tactile system, in which nerves under the surface of the skin detect touch, pressure, and other feelings; and the proprioceptive system, in which muscles, nerves, and tendons detect the location of the body in space. People with sensory issues can either have a great deal of sensitivity in these areas (for example, they will recoil from touch), or they may need a great deal of input (such as constantly swinging their body). As a result, their heightened sensory issues may interfere with their daily functioning.

  In sensory integration therapy, a physical or occupational therapist helps someone through a series of sensory and motor activities. These activities are not stressful and actually seem like games, but they are exercises that aim to help people improve their sensory functioning so it doesn't interfere as severely with daily activities. Sensory integration therapy can include wearing weighted vests, pushing heavy objects, jumping on a trampoline, hanging upside down, and listening to loud noises. Studies have shown mixed results regarding the effectiveness of sensory integration therapy, though research is still ongoing.

- **Cognitive-behavioral therapy (CBT):** CBT concentrates on helping people understand their emotions and thoughts. It allows the patient to practice effective behaviors related to regulating their own emotions, understanding and regulating symptoms and thoughts related to anxiety and depression, and developing a better understanding of others' emotions and reactions. The focus of CBT is not only on behaviors, but also on cognitions, or thoughts, that may get in the way of effective functioning in life, on the job, and in relationships with friends, family, and romantic partners. Part of the focus for adults with Asperger's might be on developing a more nuanced "theory of mind," as experts like Simon Baron-Cohen believe that people with Asperger's lack an understanding of the contents of their own and other's minds. Often, Aspies, though they are very bright, will not understand how their thoughts might be different from those of others, or what others might be feeling, and as such they may convey a lack of empathy. CBT can help Aspies develop ways to deal with their own and others' emotions and thoughts while being faithful to their personal sense of what is important and authentic. In some cases, CBT can help adults find effective coping strategies and perhaps reduce anxiety, depression, or other symptoms. In conjunction with CBT, some adults may also need medication.

Medications

So far, there are no medications specially designed to treat Asperger's or ASDs in adults or children. However, some medications are often used to treat coexisting conditions and symptoms, including depression, anxiety, OCD, and ADHD. Here are some common pharmaceutical treatments for ASDs (though your doctor may recommend others):

- **Selective serotonin reuptake inhibitors (SSRIs):** These can be used to treat anxiety and depression. This class of medication includes Prozac, Lexapro, and Zoloft. Though experts don't totally understand how these medications work, they may function in part by balancing the neurotransmitters such as serotonin in your brain. SSRIs may also work to lessen the symptoms of OCD.

> Caveat: This book does not endorse or suggest taking any particular medication, and drugs should only be taken with the advice of a doctor.

- **Antipsychotics:** Atypical antipsychotics such as Abilify and Risperdal target anxiety and illogical and negative thoughts that can lead to agitation.

- **ADD/ADHD medications:** Medications to treat ADD/ADHD include stimulants such as Ritalin, Concerta, and Adderall and nonstimulants such as Strattera. Sometimes, stimulant medications can worsen anxiety, so if anxiety is an issue for you in addition to ADD/ADHD, your doctor will have to work with both issues. Some stimulants can worsen insomnia, so talk to your doctor if that is an issue or if you find that the stimulants impact your sleep habits.

Making yourself feel better is never as simple as popping a pill into your mouth, even if you are on helpful medication. After you start taking a medication, work with your doctor regularly to let him or her know how you are feeling and what side effects you are experiencing. You should work with the doctor, being honest with yourself about how you're doing, until you've found an effective dose. This process can take a while, even months, and if you haven't found the right medication, keep trying. Even good physicians don't always know how medications will affect a particular individual. Therefore, if your medication isn't working, don't assume your doctor does not know what he or she is doing. The most important thing is that your doctor listens to you and continues working with you to find an effective medication.

HOW TO ASK FOR HELP

Realizing that you need help and asking for it are often the hardest parts of getting help. Many people go undiagnosed, and this is a terrible way to live when there are so many helpful options. Asking for help is a not a sign of being weak, deficient, or unable to run your own life. On the contrary, it's a sign of strength to recognize a problem in yourself and be willing to get help to be your best self.

Many Aspies suffer for years with anxiety and depression, not realizing there's a better life waiting for them. If you have symptoms related to anxiety and depression, you may not even realize that you need help. Check in with yourself and note if you experience any of the following telltale symptoms:

ANXIETY	DEPRESSION
■ General feeling of panic, fear, and uneasiness	■ Having a hard time concentrating, remembering details, and making choices
■ Insomnia	■ Fatigue
■ Clammy hands or feet	■ Feeling guilty for no reason, worthless, or helpless
■ Trouble breathing	■ Feeling generally pessimistic
■ Heart palpitations	■ Insomnia or oversleeping
■ Feeling agitated or fidgety	■ Loss of interest in activities you used to enjoy
■ Dry mouth	■ Consistently feeling sad or "empty"
■ Nausea	■ Thoughts of suicide, or suicide attempts
■ Tense muscles	
■ Dizziness	

Now that you're living on your own, your health is an important part of what you need to manage. Explain your symptoms to your doctor, and ask what the next steps are, such as referring you to a psychiatrist or other specialist. Let your doctor know if the symptoms persist, and don't wait for them to get too bad before you act.

Other Forms of Help

As research evolves, each year brings with it new recommended methods of helping Aspies manage their symptoms. Many of the methods are clinical, but some options, though backed by research, seem like common-sense approaches (like avoiding electronics at night to get better sleep and eating the right foods for optimal health).

- **Executive-function training:** While many adults with Asperger's have very logical minds, some have trouble with executive functions, or the ability to organize, plan, change tasks, and think flexibly. They may also struggle with attention issues that worsen their executive-function problems. One remedy is to work with an executive-function coach, who is often a learning specialist or cognitive behavioral psychologist. This person should have extensive experience working with adults who have similar issues. The goal of this type of training is to help you set up systems that enable you to effectively manage your time, work, and personal tasks. Rather than mandating that you use certain systems, the coach can (and should) work with you to develop systems that work for you. If you are interested in this type of assistance, you may want to ask your doctor for a referral to a therapist trained in CBT or executive-functioning issues.

- **Help for insomnia:** Many Aspies suffer from insomnia as children and then right into adulthood. There are several steps you can take to get the sleep you need. First, speak to your doctor about any underlying conditions, such as anxiety or depression, which may be interfering with your sleep. Your doctor might prescribe medications or recommend therapeutic treatment. Several lifestyle choices can be helpful in treating insomnia, including getting enough fresh air and exercise to help your body relax, and avoiding stimulants like caffeine before bed. In addition, you should avoid looking at television or computer screens right before bed and avoid charging phones or computers near where you sleep, as the light that these devices emit can keep you awake. Finally, keep consistent nighttime sleep rituals, and rise at roughly the same time each day to train your body about the proper times to wake up and go to sleep.

- **Exercise:** Exercise can help control irritability, anxiety, and depression, and the right kinds of exercise can also help you soothe your senses. Aspies often find that they do not enjoy games that involve teams, competition, or keeping up with others, and that's fine. Instead, exercise that involves sensory activities such as rocking or climbing might make you feel physically better, as might using exercise equipment and other solitary types of pursuits such as hiking, swimming (water is wonderful for the senses), running, martial arts, or biking. Some Aspies enjoy activities that give them proprioceptive feedback, such as lifting weights or heavy balls, and these activities can help with sensory integration training as well.

  If you are a recent high school or college graduate, you may no longer have access to free gym spaces like you did when you were in school. If working out is important to you, find a local space that isn't expensive, such as a YMCA or outdoor track, or ask your company if they have facilities for working out or offer discounts at local gyms. Some health insurance companies will also offer gym discounts or give you a small refund if you work out a given number of times.

- **Expanding your food horizons:** For Aspies, eating is not necessarily a wonderful feast for the senses. Many Aspies struggle with the texture of food because of ongoing sensory issues, making eating a healthy, well-rounded diet an elusive concept. While you likely know what a healthy diet is supposed to look like, you may be resistant to include the fruits, vegetables, and whole grains that you know you need.

How about this: Start amending your diet by adding in one or two new foods at a time rather than committing to an entirely new diet. Try blending new foods with old foods you already like. If you like pizza, try adding a vegetable you like to the pizza. If texture is a problem, make smoothies or other relatively easy-to-digest variations of foods to get your fruits and veggies. Start slowly, working your way to new foods. Build regular eating times into your schedule. While many jobs require late nights and irregular schedules, try to eat your meals at roughly the same time each day. Eating on a regular schedule makes meals more predictable for those who like their routine, and easier to digest. Try to spend meal times away from screens so you can concentrate on savoring what you're eating.

If eating a healthy diet continues to be a problem, you may want to consult a nutritionist who is sensitive to your concerns and sensory issues. They can help you find healthy foods and recipes that work with your tastes. There is a whole world of culinary delights out there, and with a little exploration, you are pretty certain to find some new foods you like. Finally, being able to tolerate—and even enjoy—a wider variety of foods will help you feel better and be more comfortable at social events that involve food.

CHAPTER 7

Answers to Common Questions

For easy reference, this chapter provides some common questions Aspies may have as they enter the adult world, look for a job, and connect with others. The answers are just one line of thinking; there are many ways to approach these scenarios and problems. As you read each answer, keep in mind that you can tweak or change the advice to suit your unique needs and approach. The answers also provide some ideas of resources and scripts you can use to resolve common issues. The common denominator? Increasing your awareness of your talents and needs and learning to advocate for yourself so those needs can be met.

Question: **I'm unsure about whether to move out of my parents' house. How do I decide whether to move out and get my own place?**

Answer: This is a difficult decision. First, examine your reasons for staying at home. Are you saving money to eventually live on your own? (This is a great reason to live with your parents for a while—but give yourself a deadline.) Or are you afraid to jump into adult life? If so, start with small steps, such as living in a dorm or with friends, or finding housing in a residential program for adults on the spectrum. Residential programs help you make a gradual transition to adult life by first placing you in a dorm or similar setting and then moving you to an independent cottage or house in a community, where adults check in regularly and help you learn important skills. You may not think it's necessary to move out of your childhood home, where you might have your meals made for you and your bills paid, but you are probably cutting yourself off from making new friends, finding a romantic partner, and living a full and satisfying life as an adult.

Question: **I have a lot of disparate skills, such as gaming and memorizing statistics, but how do I use these skills to find a job?**

Answer: Work with a career counselor at your college or high school or an independent counselor. This is a valuable resource for finding positions that use your skills. You may also want to use a career test such as the Self-Directed Search to find positions that utilize your skills and interests (see the Resources section for more information). This career inventory helps you identify potential jobs that enlist skills you have and are good at. In addition, local Asperger's support groups often offer workshops on interviewing, researching to find potential jobs, and training in job skills. Chapter 2 of this book presents some ideas of the many and varied jobs that are good for some Aspies. While these jobs may or may not be right for you, this list gives a preliminary idea of some jobs that you might start to explore by using the Internet, friends, or fellow alumni. There are countless jobs out there—some require your talents and interests—so start exploring.

Question: I am a very shy person, so how do I best prepare for a job interview?

Answer: Chapter 2 provides some common interview questions and some scripts that you can use to practice for interviews. Work through these interview questions alone or with a trusted friend or career counselor to practice your interviewing skills. While these questions may seem strange or uncomfortable at first, a little practice will help you get used to answering them and give you the tools to walk into an interview with confidence. You might want to consider interviewing for a job you don't care as much about. Even if you slip up (as most people new to interviewing do at first), you'll learn from your mistakes and be better equipped for your second interview. Practice is key to good interviewing. While you're practicing, think about some small talk you can make at the start of the interview, such as speaking about the weather or how picturesque the route was getting to the interview. Small talk should last about a minute and is a way to make a good connection with your interviewer.

Question: I feel more comfortable working from home than in an office. How can I make this accommodation work?

Answer: There are many jobs that are conducive to working remotely, although your employer may want you to occasionally work in the office. The job search is a good place to start looking for remote employment; put that in your search and you'll see the kinds of work that lend themselves to telecommuting. If working at home is very important to you, you should bring it up during the interview process. If this is really a must for you, you will probably want to confirm that it's a possibility before even going in to interview. You don't necessarily need to reveal that you have Asperger's or another form of autism spectrum disorder. You can state something along the lines of "I work best at home, where I can concentrate and be productive. I did this during my internship, and my supervisor found that I was very efficient. Could this be something I can try at this job?" You should also decide whether working at home a few times a week or month is all right for you or if you need a position that is entirely based at home. Keep in mind, however, that working at home, while peaceful and devoid of bothersome sensory and emotional input from others, can also be very isolating. If you work at home, you may need to find social or other outlets that get you out on a regular basis in order to provide that human connection.

Question: I have a history of making remarks that other people consider insensitive, though that's not at all the way I intend them to come across. How can I control this at work?

Answer: To play it safe, stay away from any comments that malign or even address a coworker's appearance, intelligence, sexual identity, gender, race, religion, or ethnic or other background. Such remarks can be interpreted not only as insensitive, but also as harassment and therefore grounds for dismissal. There is an old saying: "If you don't have something nice to say, don't say anything at all." Conversely, you can take time to think of something to say that is nice: "That color looks great on you," "Your presentation was very interesting," or "Have a nice weekend!" When you're posting comments online or sending e-mails, some simple rules of thumb can keep you out of trouble. First, stay away from remarks that disparage other people. If you need to say something, say it in person instead of sending it in an e-mail or posting it online, where it creates a permanent record. Remember the simple niceties: "Please," "Thank you," and "I appreciate your help" are all little things you can add that lend a pleasant tone to your messages. Some remarks might be interpreted as insensitive but are not likely to result in serious consequences. However, if you make a comment that you think might've been interpreted that way, find the time to apologize to the recipient in person, letting the person know it was not your intent to insult them. Simply having an awareness that you need to filter some of your remarks is a good first step. A little advance planning and self-censorship can help you avoid seeming to be insensitive or hurtful to other people.

Question: I know I have a lot to offer, but I have a hard time expressing that to other people, such as employers. How do I do so?

Answer: Many people find it difficult to talk about themselves in a positive way without fear of bragging. Work on understanding and presenting your strengths in a straightforward, humble way that you can back up with concrete evidence. For example, you can say something like, "I'm very punctual and reliable. In my internship at college, I showed up every day and never missed a deadline." If you don't know what your talents or skills are, work with a friend you trust or a career counselor to identify what you can offer and how to put your talents into the right words.

Question: People at the office are constantly going out after work, but that doesn't interest me. Is it okay if I don't go along?

Answer: It's perfectly fine to choose not to socialize at work, though there may be a few events each year you are expected to attend, such as the office holiday party. You can attend these events briefly, just making an appearance at them, but you do not need to make your social life revolve around the office. Many neurotypicals also prefer solitude or being with their own families after work. You can counter this and avoid being seen as antisocial by simply being friendly and saying hello to people in the office when you come in each day. But try to find other outlets for socializing.

Look for activities you enjoy, such as photography, learning a language, art, or dog walking, during which you can meet and socialize with people who share your interests.

Question: I really like a person I met at a party. How do I pursue this person?

Answer: If you have a friend in common, you can ask them to invite you both along to an activity so you can get to know the person better. If you participate in the same activity, this will also give you an opportunity to speak with less pressure. However, if you only know this person from the party and have their number, you can ask them out for a relaxed activity. Try to choose an activity you'll both enjoy—that will also give you material for a conversation. If the person declines your invitation, you can try one more time a few weeks later (particularly if the person says it's a busy time but indicates that another time would be better). However, that's it. Do not stalk the person or pepper them with repeated requests for a date. That behavior can be interpreted as more than insistent; it can be seen as scary, even if that's not your intent. If the person declines two invitations, look for someone else who is interested in going out with you.

Question: I am interested in becoming intimate with someone I'm dating, but I don't like touch. How do I handle this situation?

Answer: Explain your needs to the other person in a respectful and calm way. You may also need to disclose that you have Asperger's to explain why you have the needs you do. Make sure the other person understands that you find them attractive but that sometimes touch is difficult for you. You can say something like, "I like you a lot, and I would like to have physical contact with you. But I have some needs in this regard. Can I explain them to you?" A person who likes and respects you—the foundation of a good emotional and physical relationship—is likely to understand, even if they are at first disappointed. If you can, consider some other ways to be intimate. Maybe you don't like being touched, but you don't mind touching. Could you give that person a massage? And consider what types of touch you don't mind. Maybe you don't mind holding hands. Try to find ways around the issue.

Question: I would like to date people, but no one seems to match up to my standards. What do I do?

Answer: Many Aspies have an idea of the perfect partner, but these ideas are often rooted in fantasy and the imagination rather than reality. Instead of prematurely ruling out each potential partner you come across based on near-impossible standards, get to know the person a bit first. You may find that you come to like that person, warts and all. Remember you have your own imperfections, as everyone does, and that when you accept another person, including their flaws, the other person will likely accept you.

Question: After a lifetime of feeling inferior, I tend to choose romantic partners who don't treat me well and who can be abusive. How do I escape this cycle?

Answer: Research shows that you are not alone in this situation. Many Aspie women in particular tend to choose partners who flatter them but who may not treat them very well. Learn to recognize warning signs that a potential partner may be or become physically or emotionally abusive, such as flattering behavior that is overwhelming at times and that is paired with an attempt to control you and your actions. For example, if a partner tells you whom you should be friends with, what you should eat, what you should do, or even what you should read or watch on TV, this is a red-flag situation. You may have been down this road before, and you should get off it as soon as you can. Instead, find a friend who already treats you well, and perhaps explore deepening your relationship with this person into something romantic over time.

Don't rush into relationships. Instead, give yourself time to consider whether the other person makes you feel comfortable and good about yourself. While flattery is nice, don't let remarks that are intended to flatter you blind you to another person's abusive behavior. You can have it all, and you deserve it all. If you truly have felt inferior for all this time, you might really benefit from some counseling to help improve your self-esteem and confidence.

Question: I feel very awkward on dates. How can I feel more comfortable?

Answer: First of all, first dates *are* awkward. I know nobody who feels entirely comfortable on a first date. But to some degree, practice makes perfect. Jump on an online dating service or ask out an acquaintance (remember, not someone from work), and practice following good standard dating behavior, including making conversation, figuring out how to split the check, saying good night, and perhaps alluding to a "next time." The more you practice, the smoother you will become at this dating thing. If you find that you just can't make conversation, go on a date that involves an activity, such as hiking, seeing an art exhibit, bowling, or seeing a movie. During these activities, you can talk about what you're doing or seeing, giving you fodder for the conversation to flow more freely and comfortably.

You can also find a mentor—someone you like and trust who can help you think about how to plan a date and how to figure out next steps if the first date went well. Keep in mind, though, that you don't want to imitate your mentor, though it might seem natural and desirable to do so. That person has their style, and you have yours. While there's nothing wrong with getting pointers from a mentor or strategizing about how to date, find a style of doing things that feels authentic and right to you.

Question: I am really happy gaming, and I just don't feel like going out. Is that okay?

Answer: Gaming can be great fun. After all, the world of games has an understandable set of rules and predictable ways to perform well. However, gaming can be an isolating experience, and it can ultimately take over your life and become as much of an addiction as drinking, gambling, or drugs. If you think gaming has taken over your life, consider whether you have warning signs, such as the inability to be happy doing anything other than gaming or the failure to sleep or eat or groom yourself appropriately. If you think you have a problem with gaming, you may need to cut back or join a self-help group to help you cut back. Since, as in kicking any addiction, you may have to force yourself at first to stop gaming, try going out occasionally to do something else you enjoy. As time goes on, you may find that you don't need to force yourself and that going out allows you to connect with others.

Question: I have a really great friend who often asks me why I do things like repeat myself. Should I tell that person I have Asperger's?

Answer: Whether you disclose you have Asperger's is totally up to you. There is no one right answer to this question. If the person is truly a "really great friend" whom you've known for a while and trust, you might want to share this information. You can

> If you asked the other person out, especially on a first date, do not expect or mention anything about anybody but you picking up the tab. If they offer to split it, fine; and you can talk about other arrangements down the road. But today, it's yours. If they asked you, same thing: It's really on them, though you can offer to split the tab if you wish.

also simply admit to your needs and quirks without telling them you have Asperger's. Humor may help in this regard. You can say something like, "Yeah, I tend to repeat myself. Did I mention that I repeat myself? I've done it since I was little, and thanks for putting up with it."

Question: I have accepted having Asperger's and deal with it well, but I still struggle with issues such as depression, anxiety, and insomnia. Where can I turn for help?

Answer: These are common coexisting conditions among adults with Asperger's. If you are struggling with depression, anxiety, insomnia, or other psychological issues, get help today. Find a therapist who has worked with Aspie adults before and who can understand your needs and concerns and direct you to other help you may need. Please take care of yourself. Your good life is waiting.

Question: In social situations, I have spent my life imitating others to feel like I fit in. Is that wrong?

Answer: There's nothing wrong with following the behaviors of people you respect, as long as you take what they are doing and make it your own. Many Aspies, particularly Aspie women, grow up imitating unrealistic role models, such as television characters or public personalities, in order to find acceptable ways to act in social situations. These types of imitation can often wind up back-firing, as they appear fake and inauthentic to others, who really want to know you for who you are (and will like you better when you are yourself). If you need guidance, it's better to ask a trusted friend to help you strategize and to tweak their advice to make yourself feel comfortable. You can ask your friend to tell you some of the traits they like about you so you can feel confident expressing these traits in other circles. Adulthood is a time to find your authentic self, the awesome person waiting inside, who perhaps you did not feel comfortable revealing before now.

CONCLUSION

As you embark on your journey toward an independent life, you are likely full of ideas and dreams and, yes, apprehensions. It's natural. The world is changing at lightning speed and thankfully, is becoming more receptive and embracing of the challenges and unique skills of people on the spectrum. Your talents are highly adaptive for today's work world, in which your precision, technological ability, and a mind for details can help you stand ahead of the crowd. As more and more people with Asperger's or HFA enter the workplace in the years ahead, employers and society will have a greater understanding of what Aspies can offer and how to help and support these exceptional people in achieving great success.

As you go through life, try to step back and think about what you learned from each experience, even if it was painful. Everything we go through, good and bad, comes with lessons. Are there things you can do differently next time? When looking for the answer, you may need to ask for help, which is sometimes a tough thing to do. That's why having mentors and friends you trust is so important. Look for people you can reflect with, and allow them to give you feedback on what you can do differently in their hopefully supportive, nonjudgmental way. These people might be your parents, or they might be friends, colleagues, or former teachers who know you well and can help you redirect your course. Look at the strategies in this book and in the Resources section for guidance. Always feel free to tweak and change these strategies so that they suit you—you're in the driver's seat now.

IT'S HOW YOU REACT THAT COUNTS

Though you are capable of bringing immense talent to the workplace and considerable strengths to adult life, you may at times struggle, as every adult does. "It's not what happens; it's how you react that determines the life you will have"—a saying worth remembering. Your reaction to your struggles will determine whether you move forward, learning and adapting, or whether you stay still, stagnating and failing to grow. Everyone experiences setbacks, particularly when they start out in adult life. As an Aspie, you may react to failures with an inclination to give up and retreat into the comforts of childhood, including sheltering with your parents and relinquishing some of your independence. But failure is an inevitable part of experimentation, and these experiences, while painful, will help you grow.

How can you react to setbacks in a productive way? Most importantly, try not to slip into all-or-nothing thinking: *If I don't get that job, I'll never get a job,* or *If that person doesn't want to go out with me, I'll never find a romantic partner!* Instead, put each difficult situation in perspective. If you don't get one job, you will get another, perhaps just at a different company or with different responsibilities. If you weren't successful on one date, you will be successful on another; it may be cliché, but there *are* lots of fish in the sea.

When you're seeking advice, think about how you can advocate for yourself, or ask for what you need to succeed. For example, if you aren't doing well at work because your position involves too many client meetings, and you know you'd do better just working at the tasks at hand (whether it's computer programming, design, or other work) ask your supervisor in a polite and constructive way to think about revamping your job. Advocating for yourself includes making the case to your employer about why changes that will help you will also help the company. If you spend more time on tasks and less on client meetings, for example, you can be more productive. Choosing the right time to approach your employer (in other words, when the person will be receptive to what you're saying) and remaining calm while doing so are also key components of successful self-advocacy. If your company has a looming deadline to finish a product, for example, this is a good time to ask your employer if you can work rather than attend the meeting. With a deadline looming, your employer might welcome the idea of having people spend more time on task.

Self-advocacy can also be a vital part of relationships. In the past, you may have been mistreated or misunderstood. As an adult, it's critical to learn how to stand up for yourself in clear, calm, and constructive ways. If someone isn't treating you well, you need to tell them to stop, and, if they don't listen, you probably need to find another partner. You should also communicate with your partner, using and adapting some of the strategies in this book, to let them know what you need and what makes you feel comfortable and happy.

Keep in mind that growing into adulthood is a lengthy process, and it's really an evolution that never ends. You will hopefully continue to grow and change and become wiser throughout your life. That said, you may not find the perfect job, perfect partner, and great friends the minute you move out of your parents' house. However, always try to keep moving in the right direction. Think of it like this: If you start with a job that may not be ideal, you are still getting experience that will propel you to the next position. Even if one relationship doesn't work out, you've learned things about what you want and need, and what others want and need, that will help you do better the next time around. As you move through adulthood, you will accumulate experiences and wisdom that will help you achieve your considerable potential. But whether you're 20 or 90, never be afraid to think about how you can change and improve. The skills of being able to ask for help and advocating for yourself are important to this process of never-ending growth. Just remember, there may be roadblocks, but you will learn from each one. Looking back, you will amaze yourself with what you have accomplished, and looking forward, you will see a future filled with promise.

RESOURCES

Books

Attwood, Tony. *The Complete Guide to Asperger's Syndrome.* London: Jessica Kingsley, 2008.

Carley, Michael John. *Asperger's from the Inside Out: A Supportive and Practical Guide for Anyone with Asperger's Syndrome.* New York: Perigee, 2008.

Grandin, Temple. *Thinking in Pictures: My Life with Autism.* exp. ed. New York: Vintage, 2008.

Grossberg, Blythe. *Asperger's Rules!: How to Make Sense of School and Friends.* Washington, DC: Magination Press, 2012.

Robison, John Elder. *Look Me in the Eye: My Life with Asperger's.* New York: Crown, 2007.

Saperstein, Jesse. *Getting a Life with Asperger's: Lessons Learned on the Bumpy Road to Adulthood.* New York: Perigee, 2014.

Simone, Rudy. *Asperger's on the Job: Must-Have Advice for People with Asperger's or High Functioning Autism and Their Employers, Educators, and Advocates.* Arlington, TX: Future Horizons, 2010.

———. *Aspergirls: Empowering Females with Asperger Syndrome.* London: Jessica Kingsley, 2010.

Websites

AANE.org: This is the website for the Asperger/Autism Network. It "works with individuals, families, and professionals to help people with Asperger Syndrome and similar autism spectrum profiles build meaningful, connected lives . . . by providing information, education, community, support, and advocacy, all in an atmosphere of validation and respect."

Asperger-Employment.org: This is the website for the Asperger Syndrome Training and Employment Partnership. They offer a listing of job search websites and state offices of vocational rehabilitation (VR) programs.

AspergerSyndrome.org: This is the website for the Online Asperger Syndrome Information and Support (OASIS) center, which has joined with MAAP Services for Autism and Asperger Syndrome. In their words, "We've created a single resource for families, individuals, and medical professionals who deal with the challenges of Asperger Syndrome, Autism, and Pervasive Developmental Disorder/Not Otherwise Specified (PDD/NOS)." The site has a database of local support services and other kinds of help.

CookingWithAutism.com: This site provides help for parents, teachers, and people with Asperger's and other forms of autism to prepare nutritious meals. This organization also publishes a cookbook with easy-to-follow recipes broken down into manageable steps.

LimeConnect.com: Lime is a nonprofit organization that offers training, internships, and career opportunities for people with Asperger's and other disabilities.

Self-Directed-Search.com: This is the site for Self-Directed Search, a career-assessment tool.

SucceedSocially.com: A website for anyone wanting to brush up on their social skills—Aspie and neurotypical alike. Succeed Socially is "an extensive, completely free collection of articles on social skills and getting past social awkwardness."

WrongPlanet.net: Wrong Planet is a site for people with Asperger's and other forms of autism, and those with ADD and other conditions. It has a discussion forum, articles, blogging features, and how-to guides.

REFERENCES

Autism Speaks. "The 10 Best Places to Live if You Have Autism." Accessed July 16, 2015. www.autismspeaks.org/about-us/ press-releases/10-best-places-live-if-you-have-autism.

Borgman, Stephen. "How to Find Your Career on the Autism Spectrum." *Psychology Today*. July 29, 2010. www.psychologytoday.com/blog/ spectrum-solutions/201007/how-find-your-career-the-autism-spectrum.

Fastenberg, Dan. "Workers with Asperger's Syndrome Enter Economy with Challenges, Unique Gifts." *AOL Jobs*. July 19, 2012. jobs.aol.com/ articles/2012/07/19/workers-with-aspergers-syndrome-enter- workforce-in-record-numbe/.

Griswold, Alison. "Companies Are Hiring Autistic Workers to Boost the Bottom Line." *Moneybox* on *Slate*. March 28, 2014. www.slate.com/ blogs/moneybox/2014/03/28/autism_at_work_companies_like_sap_ and_freddie_mac_are_hiring_people_with.html.

Lesco, Susan. "Employment and Asperger Syndrome." Autism Research Institute. Accessed July 16, 2015. www.autism.com/advocacy_lesco.

Quora. "How Do I Communicate with a Roommate with Asperger Syndrome to Correct Inconsiderate Behavior?" Accessed July 16, 2015. www.quora.com/How-do-I-communicate-with-a-roommate-with- Asperger-Syndrome-to-correct-inconsiderate-behavior.

Shute, Nancy. "Advice for Dating with Asperger's: Don't Call 100 Times a Week." *Shots: Health News from NPR*. August 9, 2014. www.npr.org/ sections/health-shots/2014/08/08/338910290/advice-for-dating- with-aspergers-dont-call-100-times-a-week.

Silverman, Lauren. "Young Adults with Autism Can Thrive in High-Tech
Jobs." *Shots: Health News from NPR*. April 22, 2013. www.npr.org/
sections/health-shots/2013/04/22/177452578/young-adults-with-
autism-can-thrive-in-high-tech-jobs.

Singh, Maanvi. "Young Adults with Autism More Likely to Be
Unemployed, Isolated." *Shots: Health News from NPR*. April 21, 2015.
www.npr.org/sections/health-shots/2015/04/21/401243060/young-
adults-with-autism-more-likely-to-be-unemployed-isolated.

Tate, Ryan. "The Tech Industry's Asperger Problem: Affliction or Insult?"
Gawker. March 3, 2012. gawker.com/5885196/the-tech-industrys-
asperger-problem-affliction-or-insult.

Trunk, Penelope. "3 Things You Need to Know about People with Aspergers."
Penelope Trunk. October 12, 2013. blog.penelopetrunk.com/2013/10/12/
3-things-you-need-to-know-about-people-with-aspergers/.

WebMD. "Anxiety & Panic Disorders Health Center." Accessed July 16, 2015.
www.webmd.com/anxiety-panic/guide/mental-health-anxiety-disorders.

WebMD. "Depression Health Center." Accessed July 16, 2015.
www.webmd.com/depression/guide/detecting-depression.

INDEX

CPSIA information can be obtained
at www.ICGtesting.com
Printed in the USA
LVHW07*2233061018
592647LV00002B/2/P